John Barbour, John Pinkerton

The Bruce

Or, The history of Robert I. - King of Scotland

John Barbour, John Pinkerton

The Bruce

Or, The history of Robert I. - King of Scotland

ISBN/EAN: 9783743345331

Manufactured in Europe, USA, Canada, Australia, Japa

Cover: Foto ©ninafisch / pixelio.de

Manufactured and distributed by brebook publishing software (www.brebook.com)

John Barbour, John Pinkerton

The Bruce

THE BRUCE;

OR,

THE HISTORY OF ROBERT I.
KING OF SCOTLAND.

WRITTEN IN SCOTISH VERSE
By JOHN BARBOUR.

THE FIRST GENUINE EDITION,
PUBLISHED FROM A MS. DATED 1489;

WITH NOTES AND A GLOSSARY
By J. PINKERTON.

VOLUME I.

III. 347.

LONDON:

PRINTED BY H. HUGHS,
FOR G. NICOL, BOOKSELLER TO HIS MAJESTY.
M.DCC.XC.

PREFACE.

THE publication of ancient monuments of their poetry seems now to interest most nations. In France the best poets of the fifteenth century were published at Paris, in the year 1723 *. Since which time, not to mention editions of the *Roman de la Rose*, a work completed in the end of the thirteenth century, have appeared the poems of Thibaut king of Navarre, who wrote in the beginning of the thirteenth century; and the songs of Raoul de Coucy, composed in the twelfth, about the year 1190. Barbazan has also given specimens of the short romances in verse, or tales: and M. Le Grand has published a good translation of the best

---

* Oeuvres de Villon, written about 1450. Farce de l'Avocat Pathelin, about 1450. Poesies de Coquillart, 1470. Martial d'Auvergne, 1480, 2 vols. Oeuvres de Jean Marot, 1500. And the Poesies de Guillaume Cretin, 1510. Legende de Pierre Faifeu, by Bourdigne, 1531.

The works of Allain Chartier, which are large, written about 1440, were published by Du Chesne, Paris, 1617, 4to.

It is surprizing, however, that the poems of Froissart, the only poet, it is believed, France has of the fourteenth century, should still remain MS. The fifteenth century is barren of poetry in Italy and England.

he could find, from the twelfth century to the fifteenth, in 5 vols. 12mo. with prefaces, in which he shews the great superiority of these *fabliaux*, which originated in the northern parts of France, to the insipid love-songs of the Provençal troubadours, the offspring of the south; and goes so far as to say, that all the great poets, and most of the great men of France, have been born in the northern parts of that kingdom. Any reader may indeed judge, by comparing his very curious and interesting work with the account and translation of the works of the troubadours, published by l'Abbé Millot, that one of these old tales full of incident, imagination, and life, is worth all the drawling efforts of the Provençal muse, the lifeless daughter of metaphysical love.

In Spain, the late publication by Sanchez * shews that this kind of literature is not totally neglected. Italy needs not be mentioned, as the publication of her ancient poets has been constant and perpetual: but the *Filostrato* and *Teseide* of Boccace should be reprinted. In Germany diffe-

---

* This very curious work is intituled, *Coleccion de Poesias Castellanas anteriores al Siglo XV*. &c. Por D. Thomas Antonio Sanchez, Bibliotecario de S. M. En Madrid, por Don Antonio de Sancha: 1779—1782, 3 vols 8vo. published. The first volume contains the poem of the Cid; and prefixt is a letter of the marquis de Santillana, written about 1455, on the origin of Spanish poetry, with long notes by the editor, forming almost a history of Spanish poetry preceding the year 1400; and well written, if we except some oddities, as the examination whether Adam spoke first in verse or prose, &c. The Inquisition still exists in Spain! Vol. ii. contains the poems of Berceo. Vol. iii. Alexander the Great. All are accompanied with glossaries.

rent

rent productions of this sort have lately been given: and in Denmark the poetical Edda, containing the oldest Icelandic poetry, has at last appeared in print. Nor has England neglected this study, as the Reliques of Ancient English Poetry, the late excellent edition of Chaucer's Tales, and other works in this line may testify.

The poem now presented to the reader for the first time, in it's genuine ancient dress, has already gone thro' about twenty editions in Scotland since the year 1616, in which the first edition which can be discovered, was printed at Edinburgh, 12mo. But all these editions are modernized; and it was impossible to judge of the real ancient poem from them. The editor, zealous to give an edition of this interesting work, the most ancient production of the Scotish muse extant, in the very language, and orthography, of it's author, had recourse to a manuscript written in the year 1489, preserved in the Advocates' Library at Edinburgh; a collection which does great honour to that respectable society, and to their country. The society having, with much politeness, permitted a copy to be taken for publication, the editor was equally fortunate in the condescending assistance of the Earl of BUCHAN, a nobleman well known as the founder of the Scotish Society of Antiquaries; and as the friend of the ancient literature, and present welfare and honour of his country. This public-spirited peer caused the transcript to be taken under his own eye; and accompanied it with this attestation: " I David " Steuart, Earl of Buchan, have compared this " transcript of the MS. dated 1489, in the Law-
" yers'

"yers' Library at Edinburgh, with the original, "and find it to be a true copy, having corrected "such errors as I have been able to observe, in "the course of a very minute investigation and "comparison;" *(signed)* "BUCHAN:" and dated, "Edinburgh, September 27th, 1787."

The transcript, taken *literatim* from the MS. has been sent to the press, as it came; and printed from with the utmost exactness, even to the retention of small errors, which might easily have been amended. The only alteration from the original is the division into Twenty Books, with their arguments, now adopted and given for the first time; but which injures not a particle of the original text, and is an improvement, which, it is believed, every reader will approve: for the perusal of such a long work of about 12,000 verses, without any pause, or illustration, would have proved tiresome to the most patient reader; not to mention the superior clearness which such a division, and analysis, lend to a work of length, and the universal practice of ancient and modern times in such cases. It is indeed much to be wished that division, and argument, were more attended to in all publications of old language. Nævius and Ennius, the most ancient Roman poets, composed their long works in one entire piece; and antiquity has been so idle as to let us know that Lampadio first divided the poem of Nævius into books, and Vargunteius that of Ennius. Some old editor has indeed given riming titles of chapters to large divisions of this poem; but they are ill-placed, and ill-chosen: and, in spite of Mr. Hume's History, every man of reading must know that a

chapter,

chapter, or *caput*, is the proper name of a short division, properly treating of but one *head*, or incident.

The original MS. from it's orthography, appears to have been copied from one co-eval with the author; for the spelling is more barbaric, and uncouth, than that of a copy of Winton's Chronicle, written about the year 1410, in the Cotton Library. At the end of this edition the reader will find fac-similia of the MS. particularly of the colophon, which is in these words: " *Finitur codicellus de virtutibus et actibus bellicosissimi viri domini Roberti Broyss quondam Scottorum Regis illustrissimi raptim scriptus per me Johannem Ramsay ex jussu venerabilis et circumspecti viri vere magistri Symonis Lochmaleny de Ouchternunnse vicarii bene digni Anno Domini Millesimo Quadringentesimo Octuagesimo Nono.*" " Here ends the book of the virtues, and acts, of the most warlike man, the lord Robert Bruce, sometime king of Scotland, written at different times by me John Ramsay, at the command of a venerable and prudent man, and real master, Simon Lochmaleny, most worthy vicar of Ouchternunnse, in the year of our Lord One Thousand Four Hundred and Eighty-nine." The name *Lochmaleny* is so uncommon, that it seems unknown in any other Scotish record; and *Ouchternunnse* the editor cannot find. The same MS. contains the life of Wallace, by Henry the minstrel, written about 1470; and tho' it be a mere wild romance, while this poem of Barbour's is mostly real history; and far inferior in every merit to this; yet, for the sake of the language, and manners, it would be worth while to

print

print it from the MS. But this the editor muſt leave to ſome gentleman reſiding in Scotland, and curious in ſuch matters.

It is with no ſmall pleaſure that the editor has at laſt procured the genuine publication, and, by the ſpirit and liberality of the bookſeller, the elegant publication, of the oldeſt monument of the Scotiſh language. A monument which may well bear company with the beſt early poetry which any modern country can boaſt. Perhaps the editor may be accuſed of nationality, when he ſays that, taking the total merits of this work together, he prefers it to the early exertions of even the Italian muſe, to the melancholy ſublimity of Dante, and the amorous quaintneſs of Petrarca, as much as M. Le Grand does a *fabliau* to a Provençal ditty. Here indeed the reader will find few of the graces of fine poetry, little of the Attic dreſs of the muſe: but here are life, and ſpirit, and eaſe, and plain ſenſe, and pictures of real manners, and perpetual incident, and entertainment. The language is remarkably good for the time; and far ſuperior, in neatneſs and elegance, even to that of Gawin Douglas, who wrote more than a century after. But when we conſider that our author is not only the firſt poet, but the earlieſt hiſtorian of Scotland, who has entered into any detail, and from whom any view of the real ſtate and manners of the country can be had; and that the hero, whoſe life he paints ſo minutely, was a monarch equal to the greateſt of modern times; let the hiſtorical and poetical merits of his work be weighed together; and then oppoſed to thoſe of any other early poet of the preſent nations in Europe.

PREFACE.

It is indeed posterior in time to the earliest poetry of most modern nations; but it must be considered that Scotland hardly had one writer till the thirteenth century*; and this poem was written in the fourteenth. If we pass over the Slavonic nations † of Europe, whose poetry is little known; and the Celtic, and Finnish, concerning whose poetry all we know at present is, that what some regard as ancient is certainly very modern; we may consider the rest of Europe as divided into two grand languages, the Gothic of Germany, the Netherlands, and the Northern kingdoms; and the corrupted Latin of France, Spain, Italy. The English forms a medium between these two grand divisions; a circumstance which contributes much to it's energy, and richness, for it has chosen from either the words which are most expressive, and which best accord with it's genius. In the Gothic division of Europe the monuments of national poetry extend to very early times. The earliest riming poet in any modern language, as Mr. Tyrwhit remarks, is Otfrid, a German, about the year 870: from which period there are remains of

---

* See the editor's Enquiry into the History of Scotland preceding the year 1056, Part vi. chap. 2.

† Le Clerc, in his *Histoire de la Russie*, Paris, 1783, 5 vols. 4to. has in vol. iv. or i. of the modern part, given a good idea of Russian literature. Russian songs exist as old as the tenth century: they have burdens, and are much in the Asiatic style. Nestor, the first Russian historian, was born in 1056: but from 1223 till the fifteenth century, there are no Russian writers. The editor cannot specify any collection of old Russian or of Polish poetry.

German

PREFACE.

German poetry almoſt of every century *. The poetical Edda, compiled in the thirteenth century, contains ſome pieces of Scandinavian poetry ſurely as old as the ninth century. Of Anglo-Saxon, or Engliſh, poetry, a ſpecimen might be produced of every century, ſince the eighth. There is in the Cotton Library a noble ſpecimen of Anglo-Saxon poetry of the tenth century, being a romance on the wars between Denmark and Sweden; and it is much to be wiſhed that it were publiſhed, with a tranſlation. It is to be obſerved that rime is not known in Anglo-Saxon poetry till the eleventh century, as Mr. Tyrwhit ſhews: and in Scandinavian poetry, it appears not till the twelfth, as is clear from Snorro's Hiſtory, written in the thirteenth, in which numerous ſpecimens of the works of the northern ſcalds are adduced. Whether rime originated from the Arabs, among whom poetry of this kind appeared even before Mahomet, and, upon their conqueſt of Spain in the year 712 †, ſpred firſt to France, and thence to the

* Mabillon has publiſhed a beautiful German ſong, written in the year 883. See in the Memoirs of the Academy of Inſcriptions, vol. xli. an account, by the Baron Zurlauben, of a MS. containing poems by Swabian minſtrels, from about the year 1100 till 1330. But poems of the eleventh century are very rare both in Gothic and Romance.

† The Saracens did not ſeize Sicily till the year 828; and they held it for about 230 years, or till 1058. According to Creſcimbeni, the Italian poetry paſſed from the troubadours to the Sicilians. The firſt Italian poet is Ciullo d'Alcamo, a Sicilian, about the year 1200, of whom only a ſong is extant,

Roſa freſca aulentiſſima, &c.

PREFACE.

the rest of Europe, as Salmasius and Huet think; or whether it began among the monks of Italy, in the eighth century, as some others suppose; for these are the only two opinions, which now divide the literati upon this subject; certain it is that this mode of versification may be regarded as foreign to the genuine idiom of any European language, and of very late appearance in most. Whence they who believe in the riming Welch poetry, ascribed to Taliessin and other bards of the sixth century, may enjoy their own credulity.

To pass to the Southern or Latin division of Europe, the key to all the languages of which is the Latin tongue, as the key to the other half is the German, our first attention is due to France. The Latin language used in these countries may be strictly called Latin, tho' gradually corrupting, till the tenth century. About that period the Latin of different countries began to assume different forms, and to branch out into distinct and determinate dialects. It is in vain therefore to expect French, Italian, or Spanish poetry, preceding the tenth century. Nay, France can hardly shew a specimen of her poetry, preceding the twelfth cen-

---

In 1250 lived Guittone d'Arezzo. The earliest Italian romances are in prose, beginning after the year 1300: the first in verse are the *Filostrato* and *Teseide* of Boccace, about 1350. The next worth notice is the *Morgante* of Luigi Pulci, 1460. Let me here remark that Cervantes was not the first who turned the romances into ridicule. This work of Pulci, and the *Orlando Inamorato* of Berni, were written with the same intention; and in this century Carteromaco has pursued and completed the plan in his *Ricciardetto*.

tury, of which period long romances are extant; and it is surprizing that none of these genuine old romances have been published in their original dress*. Italy can, it is believed, shew little or no poetry till the thirteenth century, her poetry being borrowed, as is said, from that of the troubadours, who began about the year 1100, and continued till 1300; and the fourteenth century has Dante and Petrarca. In Spain, a country vying with Italy in every branch of literature, there is no poetry extant more ancient than the Life of Rodrigo de Bevar, more known by the epithet of the Cid, written in about 3800 long lines, by an unknown author, near sixty years after the death of that hero, or in the year 1160; and first published by Sanchez, in the year 1779. The next poet is Gonzalo de Berceo, about 1220, who wrote lives of saints, and other pious works, in stanzas of four alexandrine lines, to the same rime; a mode of

---

* *Le Roul*, or the History of Normandy, by Wace, so called from Rollo the first duke, would form about 300 pages 4to. double columns. This poet, however, gives no account of Rollo, William I. nor Richard I.; because their wars were against France. From Richard II. A. 996, he is full and curious, but fabulous. All of Rollo is;

> Ai jeo de Roul lunges cunté,
> E de sun riche parenté,
> De Normandie que il cunquist,
> E des proesces que il i fist;
> E de Guilleaume Lunge Espee,
> Auum lestoire avant menee,
> Tant que Flameng cum a felun
> Le tuerent par traisun;
> De Richard sun fiz auum dit, &c.
>
> MS. Reg. 4: c. xi.

poetry generally prevalent in Spain till the year 1400. Then follows the long poem of Alexander the Great partly tranflated from Gualter, by Juan Lorenzo of Aftorga, about the year 1250, in the fame difagreeable ftanza. In the fame century king Alfonfo the Wife wrote poems, not to mention his books of philofophy, and code of laws in profe: and in Portugal under king Dionis, himfelf the earlieft Portuguefe poet, lived Vafco Lobeira, the author of the famous romance of *Amadis de Gaula*. The profe chronicles of Spain, in Spanifh, alfo begin in this century. The fourteenth century produced in Spain Juan Ruiz, the archprieft of Hita, a pious rimer; the Jew Don Santo, a moral one; Don Juan Manuel, the biographer in verfe of the Conde Lucanor; and him of the Conde Fernan Gonzalez; Pero Gomez; the hiftorian of Alfonfo XI. in verfe; Pero Lopez de Ayala, who wrote his fatire on courts in England, in prifon; and toward the end of this, or beginning of next, century, Mofen Jordi, and Mofen Febrer. The fifteenth century has excellent Spanifh poets, Villafandino, Juan de Mena, Jorge Manrique, Aufias March, who wrote in the Valencian dialect, the famous marquis of Santillana, Diego de St. Pedro, who wrote the *Carcel de Amor*, and Juan Alonfo de Baena, who compiled the lyric poems of his predeceffors under the ufual title of *Cancionero*, MS. in the Efcurial. To this century alfo moft of the fhort Spanifh romances belong; and particularly thofe in the hiftory of the civil wars of Granada.

When we confider that the poetry of even the

moſt ſouthern, and civilized, countries of Europe begins thus lately, we ſhall rather wonder, that a country ſo remote, and diſtant from civilization, as Scotland, can boaſt of ſo reſpectable a poem as this at ſo early a period. Indeed the hero ſeems to have inſpired the author; and hardly have ever great actions been performed, without ſome author's ariſing to celebrate them. Chaucer, our poet's great cotemporary, was little known to fame, when Barbour wrote in 1375, as he tells us himſelf, B. xiii. v. 700; and he never mentions, and perhaps had not heard of, that celebrated writer. Certain it is that Chaucer afforded no model to Barbour; who ſeems to have had no ſubjects to imitate, but the old metrical romances, to which he refers. Let us not however reaſon from this that his poem is itſelf romantic; for, tho' two or three fictitious incidents are ſurely admitted in the firſt ſeven books, the truth of all, or moſt, of the reſt can be evidenced from the beſt hiſtorians, Engliſh and Scotiſh: and the reader who wiſhes to be convinced of this, without much trouble, has only to compare the hiſtory of king Robert I. in Dalrymple Lord Hailes's valuable Annals of Scotland, with our author's account. His writing in verſe is no argument againſt the veracity of his facts. In moſt countries hiſtory has firſt been written in verſe. In all countries memory is more ancient than writing; and poetry than proſe. Greece, as is well known, had early poetical hiſtorians. The poem of Nævius on the firſt Punic war, written about 238 years before Chriſt, was the earlieſt known among the Romans; and the

beginning

beginning of it puts us in mind of the harſh orthography of Barbour;

> Quei terrai Latiai hemones tuſerunt
> Vires frudeſque Poinicas fabor.—

The next poet was Ennius, who about thirty years after wrote in heroic verſe, (not in the *Saturnius*, or a kind of Iambic, as Nævius did, reſembling the ſhort quick verſe of our Barbour) the annals of Rome; and afterward the acts of Scipio Africanus. In modern Europe, the Saxon poet of the life of Charlemagne is well known, and the hiſtory of the Britons was tranſlated into French verſe from Geoffrey of Monmouth, by Wace in the twelfth century; and a hiſtory of Normandy was given by the ſame writer, in the ſame ſtyle. Not to mention the hiſtory of France in French rime of the thirteenth century; nor the Engliſh hiſtories of Robert of Gloceſter, Robert de Brunne, &c. the earlieſt native hiſtorian of Sweden is a chronicler in rime, about the year 1360. Our Winton wrote a vaſt hiſtory of the world, with Scotiſh affairs intermixt, about the year 1420, but is a bad Ennius after our excellent Nævius Barbour: tho' it be remarkable, that as Ennius omitted the firſt Punic war becauſe Nævius had written it, ſo Winton does the life of Robert I.

As to any account of our author, little can be added by the editor to what he has already ſaid in another place *, except ſome curious information,

---

* Liſt of Scotiſh poets, prefixt to Ancient Scotiſh Poems from the Maitland MS. London, 1786, p. lxxix.

from Winton's Chronicle, concerning another work of his. It being proper and neceſſary, however, to give ſome account of our poet here, it is hoped the reader will excuſe a repetition of the information formerly given, tho' not in the ſame words.

JOHN BARBOUR ſeems to have been born about the year 1326. In 1357 it appears, from a paſſport publiſhed by Rymer, dated the 13th day of Auguſt that year, that he was then archdeacon of Aberdeen. This paſſport permits him to go to Oxford, there to place three ſcholars to purſue their ſtudies, and ſcholaſtic exerciſes. By a deed, dated the 13th of September in the ſame year, alſo publiſhed by Rymer, we find our author appointed by the biſhop of Aberdeen one of his commiſſioners, to meet at Edinburgh concerning the ranſom of David II. king of Scotland, then a priſoner in England. In 1365 Rymer gives us the title of another paſſport for John Barbour, archdeacon of Aberdeen, to go thro' England, with ſix knights in company, to St. Denis, near Paris. All we find further evidenced relating to our author is that he died aged, in the year 1396, as we learn from the chartulary of Aberdeen.

He informs us himſelf, B. xiii. ver. 700, that he wrote this poem in the year 1375; and about 1440 Bower or Bowmaker, the continuator of Fordun's hiſtory of Scotland, gives him this praiſe, lib. xii. c. 9. ſpeaking of king Robert I. " *Magiſter Johannes Barbarii Archidiaconus Aberdenenſis in lingua noſtra materna, diſerte et luculenter ſatis, ipſa ejus particularia geſta, necnon multum eleganter, peroravit.*"

To

PREFACE.

To thefe particulars the editor now adds the following, from Winton's metrical chronicle, written between the years 1410 and 1420 *.

> This NINUS had ane fon alfua,
> Schir DARDANE, Lord of *Fregia*,
> Of quhome the ARCHDENE futtely
> Has maid proper Genealogie,
> Till ROBERT, our fecond king,
> That *Scotland* had in governing.
> MS. Edit. p. 63.

And fpeaking of the progrefs of the Scots from Ireland:

> Bot be the BRUTE, yitt BARBAR fayis
> Of Erifchry all uthir wayis;
> That GURGUNT BADRUK quhile was king,
> And *Brettane* had in gouerning, &c.
> p. 81.

Agreeable to Geffrey of Monmouth, lib. 1. c. 20.

Again,

> Of BRUTUS' lynnage wha will heir
> He luik the treteis that BARBEIR
> Maid intill a Genealogy,
> Reyt weil, and mair perfytly
> Than I can in any wife,
> With all my wit for til devife.
> p. 129.

---

* From a MS. in the editor's poffeffion, compared with three old ones, and prepared for the prefs by Robert Seton, 1724.

Again, speaking of Brennus and Belinus;

> Thai reid the BRUTE, and thai fall see
> Ferleis feir of thair bounté.

p. 184.

Again,

> OCTAVYUS than into thai dayis
> As of BRUTE the storye sayis,
> Of all *Brettane* haill was king.

p. 329.

The following passage, not immediately to the purpose, is inserted on account of its singularity:

> Bot of the BRUTE the storye sayis
> That LUCIUS HYBER in his dayis
> Was of the hie stait procuratour,
> Nouthir callit king na empryour.
> Fra blayme wes than the author quyte,
> As he before him fand, to wryte;
> And men of gude discretioun
> Suld excuse and loiff HUCHEONE,
> That cunnand was in literature.
> He maid a gret gest of ARTHURE:
> And the awenturis of GAWANE:
> And the 'pistill als of sueit SUSANE.
> He was curious in his style,
> Fayr, and facund, and subtile,
> And ay to plesance had delyte;
> And maid in metyr meit his dyte,
> Littill or nocht neverthelefs
> Wawerand fra the suthfastnes.
> Had he callit LUCIUS procuratour,
> Qhair that he callit him empryour, &c.

p. 364.

And

PREFACE. xxi

And HUCHONE of the *Aule Ryall*
Intill his geft hiftoriall.   *Ib.*

Sen HUCHEONE of the *Awle Ryall*
Intill his geft hiftoricall.   *Ib.*

HUCHEONE baith, and the author.   *Ib.*

There is every reafon to believe that the BRUTE, in the paffages above quoted, after p. 184, is quite different from Barbour's Genealogy of the kings of Scotland, in which the lineage of Brutus was given, as appears from the paffage p. 129, above: and is either Geffrey of Monmouth's book, or Wace's *Le Brut*. Of Hutcheon the editor knows nothing. He once fufpected that the fhort hiftory of Scotland, in profe, down to the end of Robert the Second's reign, to be found at the end of Winton, and which is a curious remain of old Scotifh profe, was the book of Barbour above mentioned; but there is no mention of Dardanus or of Brutus in it: and he believes that Barbour's work is loft.

To return to the prefent work, Winton not only repeatedly quotes it, but omits the whole reign of Robert I. as Barbour had already written it in the fame metre which he ufes.

In book viii. chap. 139, p. 601, Winton begins to give long extracts from Barbour's poem. He there prefents us with an extract from B. i. ver. 37—170. After a long and often fabulous account of the controverfy between Baliol and Bruce, and the fentence of Edward, he fays, p. 627,

> Bot luik quhat followit eftirwart;
> How ROBERT our king recoverit his land,
> That occupyit with his fayis he fand;

And

>And it reſtoryt in all fredome,
>Quyt till his airis of all thraledome;
>Quha that lykis that till witt
>To the BRUYSE' buke I thaim remitt.
>Quhair maiſter JOHNNE BARBEIR, Archdene
>Of *Aberdene*, as mony has ſeyne,
>His deidis deitit mair vertuuſly,
>Than I can think in all ſtudy;
>Haldand in all leill ſuthfaſtnes,
>Set all he wrait nocht his prowes.

Winton then gives an account of the Cummins, and of the Bruces, and of the affairs of Scotland down to the year 1304, at which year, p. 680, he ſays,

>The Archdekin in BRUCES buke, &c.

and quotes B. i. ver. 187, &c. Then in p. 682 he gives another extract from B. i. ver. 483, to B. ii. ver. 36, with ſlight omiſſions, additions, and alterations. After which, p. 686, he ſays,

>Quhat eftir this the BRUCE ROBERT
>In all his tyme did eſtirwert,
>The Archdene of *Abirdene*
>In BRUCE's buke has gart be ſene,
>Mair wyſlie tretit into wryte,
>Than I can think in all my wyte.
>Thairfore I will now thus lychtly
>Ourpaſs att this tyme his ſtory.

Winton then, chap. 157, excuſes the lameneſs of his work, and recapitulates the years till David II.: chap 158 has the betraying of Wallace by Menteith, 1305; and the dedication of the new cathedral of St. Andrews, 1318; both very briefly told.

PREFACE. xxiii

told. Chap. 159 bears the birth of king David II. 1320, and the depofition of Edward II. of England, 1326, by his reckoning. Chap. 160 gives the wedding of David II. 1328, and the death of Robert I. Chap. 161 begins the reign of David II. at length. Tho' Winton's work will not bear a total publication, it would be worth while to publifh this latter part, from David II. till 1414, as forming with Barbour a chain of memoirs in Scotifh verfe, for the hiftory of Scotland, almoft down to the commencement of our memoirs in Scotifh profe, in the hiftory of Lindfay of Pittfcottie. The fpace from 1414 till 1437, when Lindfay begins, might be fupplied from Bellenden's tranflation of Boethius, which varies from the original, and of which Lindfay's work was meant to be a continuation, as we learn from himfelf. This part of Winton and Bellenden would form two large octavo volumes.

This preface fhall be clofed with one little remark, to wit, that the name of THE BRUCE is given to this poem, as its genuine ancient name, as appears from the lift of ancient Scotifh poems in Wedderburn's Complaint of Scotland, 1549, and from the above paffages of Winton *.

* It is worth obfervation that, tho' the edition of this work 1616 be the oldeft difcovered, yet there muft have been at leaft one more ancient: for Gordon, in his *Hiftorie of Bruce*, a poem printed at Dort 1615, 4to. mentions this poem, as " the old printed book," in his preface; where he alfo fpeaks of a MS. on vellum, containing a poetical life of Bruce by Peter Fenton, a monk of Melrofe, written in 1369; from which he borrows fome incidents. It ended, as Gordon's, with the battle of Bannocburn. The MS. belonged to Donald Farquharfon.

ENNIUM SICUT SACROS VETUSTATE LUCOS
ADOREMUS, IN QUIBUS GRANDIA ET ANTIQUA
ROBORA NON TANTAM HABENT SPECIEM,
QUANTAM RELIGIONEM.

QUINTILIAN.

THE
BRUCE.

BUKE I.

Vol. I.   B

ARGUMENT.

Proeme. — Stait of Scotland at the deth of ALEXANDER III.—*Storie of* DOUGLAS.—*The historie beginis with the cunand maid between* ROBERT DE BRUYSE, *afterward King, and Schir* JOHN CUMIN.—*Traitory of* CUMIN, *quha betrays* ROBERT *til* EDWARD I. *of England.*

THE BRUCE.

BUKE I.

STORYSE to rede ar delitabill,
Suppofe that thai be nought but fabill;
Than fuld ftoryfe that futhfaft wer,
And thai war faid on gud maner,
Have doubill plefance in herying. 5
The fyrft plefance is thair carping,
And the 'tothir thair futhfaftnes,
That fchewys the thing rycht as it was;
And fuch thyngs that ar likand
Tyll manys herying ar plefand. 10
Thairfor I wald fayne fet my will,
Giff my wyt mycht fuffice thairtill,
To put in wryt a futhfaft ftory
That it laft ay furth in memory

Swa

Swa that na tyme of lenth it let, 15
Nor ger it haly be forget.
For auld ſtoryſe, that men redys,
Repraiſents to thaim the dedys
Of ſtalwart folk, that lywyt ar,
Rycht as thai than in preſence war. 20
And certes thai ſuld weill have pryſe
That in thair tyme war wyght and wyſe;
And led thair lyff in gret trawaill,
And oft, in hard ſtour of bataill,
Wan rycht gret price off chewalry, 25
And war woydyt off cowardy.
As was King ROBERT off Scotland,
That hardy was of hart and hand,
And gud Schyr JAMES OFF DOUGLAS,
That in hys tyme ſa worthy was, 30
That off hys price, and hys bounté,
Into far lands renownyt waſe he.
Off thaim I thynk this Buk to ma:
Now God gyff grace that I may ſwa
Tret it, and bryng it till endying, 35
That I ſay nought bot ſuthfaſt thing.

When ALEXANDER the King was deid,
That *Scotland* haid to ſteyr and leid,

Ver. 37. Alexander III. died 16 March 1286. Margaret his grand-daughter reigned till 1290: an inter-regnum followed, till 30 November 1292, when John Baliol was crowned; who was depoſed by Edward I. of England, in 1296. Another inter-regnum ſucceeded, till 27 March 1306, when Robert the Great, the hero of this poem, aſcended the throne.

The

The land fax yer, and moyr perfay,
Ley defolat after hys day. 40
Till that the Barnage at the laft
Affemblyt thaim, and fayndyt faft
To choyfe a king, thair land to fter,
That off awnceftry cumyn wer
Off kings, that aucht that roawtie, 45
And mayft had rycht thair king to be.
Bot Enwy, that is fa feloune,
Maid amang thaim great defcenfeoun,
For fum wald haiff the BALLEOLL king,
For he was cumyn off the offspryng 50
Off hyr that eldeft fyftir was.
And othir fum nyt all that cafe;
And faid that he thair king fuld be
That war in als ner degre,
And cumyn war of the neift male, 55
And in branch collaterale:
Thai faid fucceffion of kyngrik
Was nocht to lawer feys lik;
For ther mycht fucced na female,
Quhill foundyn mycht be ony male, 60
Thow that in hir ewyn defcendand,
Thai bar all other wayis on hand;
For than the neyft cumyn off the feid,
Man or woman, fuld fucceid.

Ver. 61, 62. *Sic* MS.—Editions read, with equal obfcurity,
That were in line even defcendand;
They bear all otherwife in hand.

Be this refoun that part thought hale, 65
That the Lord of *Anandyrdale*,
ROBERT the BRWYSE Erle off *Carryk*,
Oucht to fucceid to the kynryk.
The Barownys thus war al difcord,
That on na maner mycht accord: 70
Till at the laft thai all concordyt,
That all thair fpek fuld be recordyt
Till Schyr EDUUARD off *Yngland* King,
And he fuld fwer that, bot fenyeyng,
He fuld that arbyter difclar, 75
Of thir twa that I tauld off ar,
Quhilk fucceid to fick a hycht,
And lat him ryng that had the rycht.
This ordynance thaim thocht the beft,
For at that tyme was pefe and reft 80

Ver. 68. David Earl of Huntingdon, grandfon of David I. was the fource of the claimants, Baliol and Bruce. The former was grandfon of Margaret, eldeft daughter of Earl David; the latter was fon of Ifabella, the fecond daughter. Sir David Dalrymple, to whofe valuable labours on Scotifh hiftory thefe notes will often be indebted, has fhewn that Baliol was undoubtedly the legal heir of the Scotifh crown. Barbour, in fpeaking of Bruce as the male heir only, oppofes him to Dervorgil, the mother of Baliol, who was alive. Baliol was fon of Dervorgil, daughter of Margaret, daughter of Earl David. Bruce was fon of Ifabella. But it is clear that Margaret, and her daughter Dervorgil, and their defcendants, muft have enjoyed the crown before Ifabella, or any of her defcendants. Robert Bruce, Earl of Carrick, competitor with John Baliol, was grandfather of our hero.

Betwyx

Betwyx *Scotland* and *Yngland* bath,
And thai couth not perſawe the ſkaith,
That towart thaim was apperand;
For that as the King off *Yngland*
Held ſwylk freyndſhip, and cumpany   85
To thair king, that was ſwa worthy,
Thai trowyt that he, as gud nyghbur,
And as freyndſome compoſitur,
Wald hawe jugyt in lawté.
Bot otherwayis all yheid the gle.   90

A! blynd folk full off all foly!
Haid ye unbethocht you enkerly,
Quhat perell to you mycht apper,
Ye had not wrocht on that maner.
Haid ye tane keip how at that King   95
Alwayes, forowtyn ſojournying,
Trawayllyt for to wyn ſenyhory,
And throw his mycht till occupy
Lands, that war till him marcheand,
As *Walis* was, and als *Ireland*;   100
That he put to ſwylk thrillage,
That thai, that war off hey perage,
Suld ryn on fute, as rebaldaill.
Quhan he wald our folk aſſaill
Durſt nane of *Walis* in bataill ride,   105
Nor yhet fra ewyn fell abyd,
Caſtell or wallyt toune within,
That he ne ſuld lyff and lymys tyne.

Into fwilk thrillage thaim held he,
That he ourcome throw his powfté. 110
Ye mycht fe he fuld occupy
Throw flycht, that he ne mycht throw maiftiry.
Had ye tane kep quhat was thrillage,
And had confideryet hys ufage,
That grypyt ay, bot gayne gevyng, 115
Ye fuld, forowtyn his demyng,
Haff chofyn yow a king, that mycht
Have haldyn veyle the land in rycht.
Walys enfample mycht have bein
To yow, had ye it forowfein, 120
That be othir will him chafty,
And wyfe men fayes he is happy.
For unfayr things may fall perfay,
Alfe weill to morn, as yhiftirday.
Bot ye traiftyet in lawté, 125
As fympile folk, but malvyté,
And wyft not quhat fuld eftir tyd:
For in this warld that is fa wyde,
Is nane determynat that fall
Knaw things that ar to fall, 130
Bot God, that is off maift powefté,
Refewyt till his maiefté,
For to knaw, in his prefcience,
Off allryn tyme the mowence.

In this maner affentyt war 135
The Barowns, as I faid you ar.

And

And throch thair aller hale aſſent,
Meſſingers till hym thai ſent,
That was than in the haly land,
On *Saraceny's* warrayand.   140
And fra he wyſt quhat charge thai had,
He buſkyt hym, but mar abad,
And left purpos that he had tane;
And till *Ingland* agayne is gane.
And ſyne till *Scotland* word ſend he,   145
That thai ſuld mak ane aſſemblé,
And he in hy ſuld cum to do
In all things, as thai wrayt him to.
Bot he thocht weill, throuch thair debate,
That he ſuld ſlely fynd the gate   150
How that he all the ſenyhowry,
Throw his gret mycht, ſuld occupy.
And to ROBERT the BRWYCE ſaid he,
" Gyff yow will hald in cheyff off me,
" For evirmar, and thyne offſpryng,   155
" I ſall do ſwa yow ſall be king."
' Schyr,' ſaid he, ' ſa God me ſave,
' The kynryk I yharn I not to have,
' Bot gyff it fall off rycht to me;
' And gyff God will that it ſa be;   160
' I ſall als frely in all thing
' Hald it, as it affer to king.

Ver. 139. A miſtake. Edward was in England. He returned from the Holy Land in 1272, or eighteen years before this time.

' Or

'Or as myn eldrs forouch me
'Hald it in freyaſt rowaté.'
The tothir wreyth him, and ſwar 165
That he ſuld have it nivir mar:
And turnyt him in wreth away.
Bot Schyr IHON the BALLEOLL perſay
Aſſentyt till him, in all his will,
Quharthrouch fell eftir mickill ill. 170
He was king bot a little quhile,
And throuch gret ſutelté and ghyle,
For litill encheſone, or nane,
He was areſtyt ſyne and tane.
And degradyt ſyne was he 175
Off honour and off dignité.
Quhythir it was throuch wrang or rycht,
God wat it, that is maiſt off mycht.

Quhan Schyr EDOUARD, the mychty King,
Had on this wyſe done his likyng 180
Off JHONE the BALLEOLL, that ſwa ſone
Was all defawtyt and undone,
To *Scotland* went he than in hy,
And all the land gan occupy:
Sa hale that bath caſtell and toune 185
War intill his poſſeſſione,
Fra *Weik* anent *Orkenay*,
To *Mullyrſnwk* in *Gallaway*.
And ſtuffyt all with *Ingliſe* men;
Schyrreffys and bailyheys maid he thain, 190

Ver. 183. July 1296.

And

And allryn othir officers,
That for to gowern land affers,
He maid of *Inglis* nation.
That worthyt than fa rych fellone,
And fa wykkyt, and cowatoufe,   195
And fwa hawtane, and difpitoufe,
That *Scottsmen* mycht do nathing
That ever mycht pleyfe to thair liking.
Thair wyffs wald thai oft forly,
And thair dochtrys difpitufly;   200
And gyff ony off thaim thairat war wrath,
Thai watyt hym wele with gret fkaith.
For thai fuld fynd fone enchefone,
To put him to deftructione.
And gyff that ony man thaim by   205
Had ony thing that was worthy,
As horfe, or hund, or othir thing,
That war plefand to thair liking,
With rycht or wrang it have wald thai.
And gyff ony wald thai withfay,   210
Thai fuld fwa do, that thai fuld tyne
Othir land, or lyff, or leyff in pine.

Ver. 195. Edward I. was a brave and warlike prince, yet had the innate cruelty of a favage; fo that the maxim, that cowards are always cruel, will not bear to be reverfed. This cruelty was a part of his difpofition, not of his politics: for nothing can be more impolitic in a conqueror than cruelty; as the Roman empire, which ftood upon clemency, and many other examples on both fides, prove. Scotland might perhaps have remained annexed to England, if Edward had even had political clemency.

For thai dempt thaim eftir thair will,
Takand na kep to rycht, na fkill.
A quhat thai dempt thaim felonly! 215
For gud knychts that war worthy,
For litill enchefowne, or than nane,
Thai hangyt be the nek-bane.
Als that folk, that evir was fre,
And in fredome wount for to be, 220
Throw thair gret myfchance, and foly,
War tretyt than fa wykkytly,
That their fays thair jugis war;
Quhat wrechitnes may man have mar?

A! fredome is a nobill thing! 225
Fredome mayfe man to haiff liking;
Fredome all folace to man giffis:
He levys at efe, that frely levys!
A noble hart may haiff nane efe,
Na ellys nocht that may him plefe, 230
Gyff fredome failyhe: for fre liking
Is yharnyt our all othir thing.
Na he, that ay hafe levyt fre,
May nocht knaw weill the propyrté,
The angyr, na the wrechyt dome, 235
That is cowplyt to foule thyrldome.
Bot gyff he had affayit it,
Than all perquer he fuld it wyt;

Ver. 225. Our poet here gives into a moving digreffion, in praife of liberty; and expofes, in ftriking colours, the miferies of flavery.

And

And fuld think fredome mar to pryfe,
Than all the gold in warld that is. 240
Thus contrar things evirmar,
Difcoweryngs off the tothir ar.
And he that thryll is has not his;
All that he hafe enbandownyt is
Till hys lord, quhatevir he be. 245
Yheyt hafe he not fa mekill fre
As fre wyll to leyve, or de,
That at hys hart hym draws to dre.
Than mayfe clerks queftioun,
Quhen thai fall in difputatioun, 250
That gyff man bad hys thryll oucht do,
And in the famyn tyme come hym to
His wyff, and afkyt hym hyr det,
Quhithir he hys lords neid fuld bet,
And pay fryft that he owcht, and fyne 255
Do furth hys lords commandyne;
Or leve onpayit hys wyff, and do
The things that commandyt is hym to.
I leve all the folutioun
Till thaim that ar off mar renoun. 260
Bot fen thai mak fic competying
Betwixt the detts off wedding,
And lords bidding till hys thrill,
Ye may weile fe, thoucht nane you tell,
How hard a thing that thryldome is. 265
For men may weile fe, that ar wyfe,
That wedding is the hardeft band,
That ony man may tak on hand.

And

And thryldom is weill wer than deid,
For quhill a thryll his lyff may leid, 270
It mervys him, body and banys,
And dede anoyis him bot anys:
Schortly to say is nane can tell
The halle conditioun off a thryll.

This gat levyt thai, and in sic thryllage 275
Bath pur, and thai off hey perage.
For off the lords sum thai slew;
And sum thai hangyt, and sum thai drew:
And sum thai put in presoune,
Forowtyn cause, or enchesoune. 280
And amang others off DOUGLASE
Put in presoune WILYAM wase,
That off DOUGLASE wase Lord and Syr.
Off him thai makyt a martyr;
Fra thai in presoune him sleuch, 285
His lands that fayr inewch,
Thai the Lord off *Clyffurd* gave.
He had a sone, a litill knave,

That

Ver. 281. There was no Earl of this great family till 1357. *Annals of Scotland*, II. 224. Barbour uses *Syr* for *Lord*, being a contraction of *Seigneur*. Our application of *Sir* to knights only is of modern date: and anciently even priests had the *Sir*, a translation of *Dominus*, implying either Lord or Master. The chiefs of Douglas were barons; and the title of *Sir* prefixt to their names, and to others by modern writers, following the ancient, is improper, because that prefixture now belongs to knights only, whereas in ancient times even kings had it; *Schir Edward the nobil King*. Baron William

That was than bot a litill page;
Bot fyne he was off gret waflage, 290
His fadyrs dede he wengyt fua,
That in *Ingland*, I underta,
Was nane off lyve that him ne dred;
For he fa fele off harnys fched,
That nane that lyvys thaim can tell: 295
Bot wondirly hard thing fell
Till him, or he till ftate was brocht.
Thair was nane aventur that mocht
Stunay his hart, na ger him let
To do the thing that he wer on fet; 300
For he thocht ay entirly
To do his deid awyfely.
He thocht weill he wis worth na feyle,
That mycht of nane anoyis feyle;
And als for till efcheve gret things, 305
And hard trewalys, and bargangings,
That fuld ger his price dowblyt be.
Quhairfor, in all his lyvetyme, he

William Douglas was the firft nobleman who joined Wallace, May 1297, in the heroic attempt to free his country, overrun in 1296 by Edward I. an attempt utterly ruined at Falkirk, July 1298: fo that Wallace's progrefs was terminated in a twelve-month, or fo; and Henry's poem on him is but the hiftory of two years, while this of Barbour embraces twenty-four. Wallace was taken, and beheaded, 1304—5; but William Douglas had deferted him, Auguft 1297, and yielded himfelf prifoner to Edward I. *Annals*, I. 249. Baron James Douglas, whofe deeds grace this poem, was his fon.

Was

Was in gret payn, and gret trewaill,
And nivir wald for myfcheiff faill,   310
Bot dryve the thing rycht to the end,
And tak the ure that God wald fend.
His name was JAMES OF DOUGLAS:
And quhen he herd his fadyr was
Put in prefoune fa fellounly,   315
And a his lands halyly
War gevyn to the CLYFFURD perfay,
He wyft not quhat to do na fay;
For he had natthing for to difpend,
Na thair was nane that evir kend   320
Wald do fa mekill for him, that he
Mycht fufficiantly fundyn be.
Than wis he wondir will off wane,
And fodanly in hart has tane,
That he wald trewail our the fe,   325
And a quhile in *Paryfe* be,
And dre myfcheiff quhar nane him kend,
Till God fum fuccours till him fend.
And as he thocht he did rycht fua,
And fone to *Paryfe* can he ga,   330
And levyt thair full fympolly,
The quhair he glaid was and joly;
And till fwylk thowtefnes he yeid,
As the courfe afks off yowtheid.
And umquhill into rybbaldaill,   335
And that may mony tyme awaill,
For knawlage off mony ftats,
May quhile awailye full mony gats.

As

BUKE I.

As to the gud Erle off A<small>RTAYIS</small>
R<small>OBERT</small>, befell in his dayis.   340
For oft feynyeyng off rybbaldy
Awailyeit him, and that gretly.
And *Catone* sayis us, in his wryt,
That to fenyhe foly quhile is wyt.
In *Paryſe* ner thre yer duellyt he;   345
And then come tythands our the ſe,
That his fadyr was done to ded.
Then wis he wa, and will of red;
And thocht that he wald hame agayne,
To luk gyff he, throw ony payn,   350
Mycht wyn agayn his heretage,
And his men out off all thryllage.
To *Saint Androws* he come in hy,
Quhar the Byſchop full curtaſly.
Reſavyt him, and gert him wer   355
His knyvys forouch him to ſcher;
And cled him rycht honorabilly,
And gert ordayn quhar he ſuld ly.
A weile gret quhile thair dwellyt he;
All men lufyt him for his bounté;   360
For he was off full fayr effer,
Wyſe, curtaiſe, and deboner;
Larg, and luffand, als was he,
And our all things luffyt lawté.

Ver. 339. Two Roberts, Earls of Artois, are famous; R. I. 1237, R. II. 1250. It ſeems uncertain to which our author alludes.

Ver. 353. William of Lamberton.

Lawté to luff is gret wily, 365
Throuch lawté liffs men rycht wifly;
With a wertu, and lawté,
A man may yeit sufficyand be.
And but lawté may nane haiff pryse,
Quhither he be wycht, or he be wyse; 370
For quhar it failyeys, na wertu
May be off price, na off valu,
To mak a man sa gud, that he
May symply callyt gud man be.

He was in all his deds lele, 375
For him dedeynyeit not to dele
With trechery, na with falset.
His hart on hey honour wis set:
And him cuntentyt on sic maner,
That all him luffyt that war him ner: 380
Bot he was not sa fayr, that we
Suld spek gretly off his beauté;
In wysage wis he sum deill gray,
And had black har, as I hard say;
Bot off lymys he wis weill maid, 385
With banys gret, and schuldrys braid.
His body war weill maid, and lenye,
As thai that saw him said to me.
Quhen he wis blyth he wis lusty,
And meyk, and sweyt in cumpany. 390

Ver. 390. Does Mr. Home allude to this passage, in his admirable tragedy of Douglas?
———————mild with the mild,
But with the froward he was fierce as fire.

Bot

Bot quha in battaill mycht him se
Anothir cuntenance had he.
And in fpek ulifpyt he fum deill;
Bot that fat him rycht wondre weill.
Till gud ECTOR of *Troy* mycht he 395
In mony things liknyt be:
ECTOR had blak har as he had,
And ftark lymys, and rycht weill maid,
And ulyfpit alfua as did he,
And wis fulfillyt in leavté; 400
And wis curtaife, and wyfe, and wycht.
Bot off manheid, and mekill mycht,
Till ECTOR dar I nane comper,
Off all that evir in warldys wer.
For in hys tyme fa wrocht he, 405
That he fuld gretly luvyt be.

He duellyt thair, quhill on a tid,
The King EDUUARD, with mekill prid,
Come to *Strevillyne* with gret mengye,
For till hald thair ane effemble. 410
Thyddirwart went mony barowne,
Byfchop WYLYAME off LAMBYRTOUNE
Reid thyddyr als, and with him was
This Squyer IAMIS of DOWGLAS.
The Byfchop led him to the King, 415
And faid, " Scheyr, I to you bryng

Ver. 412. For the actions of this double and defigning prelate, fee *Annals of Scotland*.

" This child, that clemys your man to be,
" And prays you per cheryté,
" That ye refave his homage
" And grants him his heretage."   420
' Quhat lands clemys he ?' faid the King.
" Schyr, gyff that it be your liking,
" He clemys the lordfchip off *Douglas*,
" For lord thiroff hys faddyr was."
The King then wrethyt him entirly,   425
And faid, ' Schyr Byfcnop, fekyrly
' Gyff you wald kep ye fewté,
' Yow maid nane fic fpeking to me.
' His faddyr ay wis my fay feloune,
' And deyt thairfor in my prefoun,   430
' And wis agayne my Maiefté:
' Quharfor hys ayr I aucht to be.
' Ga purchis land quhar eir he may,
' For thairoff haffys he nane perfay;

Ver. 417. *Child* was a term for a *Damoifeau*, or noble youth, before he was knighted. Whence *Horn Child*, an old Englifh romance; and *Child Maurice*, a fine Scotifh ballad. The later is fometimes called *Gil Maurice*; and *Gil* has the fame meaning, tho' now ufed for *child* in the Buchan dialect. *Gil* in proper names is Gothic, not Irifh, as fome imagine: *Gilimer*, *Gilbert*, &c. &c. are known Gothic names. So our Gillies, *filius Jefu*; Gilchrift, *filius Chrifti*; Gilbride, *filius Brigidæ*, and others. The Irifh is full of Gothic words, becaufe the Danes and Norwegians fettled in Ireland, and our highlands: but no Irifh ever went to Scandinavia.

'The CLYFFURD fall thaim haiff, for he   435
'Ay lely has ferwyt to me.'

The Byfchop hard him fwa anfuer,
And durft than fpek till him na mar;
Bot fra hys prefence went in hy,
For he dred fayr his felouny: 440
Swa that he na mar fpak thairto.
The King did that he com to do;
And went till *Ingland* fyn agayn,
With mony man of mekill mayn.

LORDINGS! QUHA LIKS FOR TILL HER, 445
THE ROMANYS NOW BEGYNYS HER,

Ver. 446. This word *Romanys* does not mean what we now term a *romance*, or fiction; but a narration of facts in romance, or the *vulgar tongue*. This ufe of the term is the genuine one, while we abufe it. Decrees of councils, and other remains of the ninth and tenth centuries in France, fhew that the Francic, or German, was the court language; while the common people fpoke the *lingua Romana ruftica*, or romance. When this laft language had prevailed, as that of the greater number always does, and began to be written, it was long called *romance*, but laterly *French*. Such was alfo the cafe in Spain and Italy. See *Hift. de la langue Franc.* prefixed to the *Poefies du Roi de Navarre*, Paris 1742. As tales were firft written in romance, the name of the language paffed to the fubject. Barbour begins, ver. 8, &c. with telling us, that his narration is *futhfaft*, or true: and the reader needs only perufe *Dalrymple's Annals*, to fee the veracity of moft, if not all of it.

Off men that war in gret diſtreſs,
And aſſayit full gret hardynes,
Or thai mycht cum till thair entent;
Bot ſyne our Lord ſic grace thaim ſent,   450
That thai ſyne, throw thair gret walour,
Come till gret hycht, and till honour,
Magre thair foyis ivir ilk ane,
That war ſa fele, that ane till ane
Off thaim thai war weill a thouſand;   455
Bot quhar God holpys quhat may withſtand?
Botand we ſay the ſuthfaſtnes,
Thai war ſum tyme ev'n mar than les;
Bot God that maiſt is off all mycht,
Preſerwyt thaim in hys forſycht,   460
To weng the harme, and the contrer,
All that fele folk and pantener
Dyd till ſympill folk and worthy,
That couth not help thaimſelfs forthy.
Thai war lik to the *Machabeys*,   465
That, as men in the Bibell ſeys,
Throw thair gret worſchip and walour,
Faucht into mony ſtallwart ſtour,
For to delyvir thair countré
Fra folk that, throw iniquité,   470

Ver. 458. As being not only few, but diſcomfited, divided, diſpirited.

Ver. 462. The editions read:
 To venge the harmes, and the contrares,
 That they fell folk and oppreſſares.

Hald

Hald thaim and thairs in thrillage:
Thai wroucht fua throw their waffelage,
That, with few folk thai had victory
Off mychty Kings, as fayis the ftory,
And delyveryt thair land all fre; 475
Quharfor thair name fuld lovyt be.

This Lord the BRWYSE I fpak of ayr,
Saw all the kynryk fwa forfayr,
And fwa trawlyt the folk faw he,
That he thairoff had gret pité. 480
Bot quhat pité that e'er he had
Na cuntenance thairoff he maid,
Till on a tyme Schyr IHONE CUMIN,
As thai come ridand fra *Strewillyn*,
Said till hym, ' Schyr, will ye not fe, 485
' How that gowernyt is thys countré?
' Thai fla our folk, but enchefoune,
' And hald thys land agayne refoune,
' And ye thairoff fuld lord be;
' And gyff that ye will trow to me, 490
' Ye fall ger mak thairoff king,
' And I fall be in your helping:
' With thy ye giff me all the land,
' That ye haiff now intill your hand;
' And gyff that ye will not do fua, 495
' Na fwylk a ftate upon you ta,

Ver. 483. John Cumin, of Badenoch, a branch of the powerful family of Cumin; as was the earl of Buchan at this time.

' All

'All hale my land fall yours be;
'And lat me ta the ftate on me:
'And bring thys land out of thyrllage.
'For thair is nothir man, na page,   500
'In all thys land bot thai fall be
'Fayn to mak thaimfelvys fre.'
The Lord the BRWISE hard hys carping,
And wend he fpak bot futhfaft thing.
And, for it likit till his will,   505
He gave his affent fone thairtill:
And faid, " Sen ye will it be fwa,
" I will blythly upon me ta
" The ftate, for I wate that I have rycht;
" And rycht mayfe oft the feble wycht."   510

The Barownys than accordyt ar,
And that ilk nycht writyn war
Thair endenturs, and athyis maid,
To hald that thai forfpokyn haid.

Bot off all things wa worth trefoune!   515
For thair is nothir duk ne baroune,
Na erle na prynce, na king off mycht,
Thoch he be nivir fa wyfe na wicht,
For wyt, worfchip, price, na renoun,
That ivir may wauch hym with trefoune.   520
Wis not all *Troy* with trefoune tane,
Quhen ten yers off the wer wis gane?
Thain flayn wis moné thoufand
Off thaim withowt, throw ftrenth of hand;

As

As Dares in hys buk he wrate, 525
And Dyts that knew all thair ſtate,
Thai mycht not haiff beyn tane throw mycht,
Bot treſoune tuk them throw hyr flycht.
And Alexandir the Conquerowr,
That conqueryt *Babylonys* tour, 530
And all this warld off lenth and breid,
In twal yher, throw his douchty deid,
Wis ſyne deſtroyit throw puſoune,
In hys awyne houſe, throw gret treſoune.
Bot or he deit hys land delt he; 535
To ſe hys dede wis gret pité.
Julus Cesar als that wan
Bretane and *Fraunce*, as douchty man,
Affryk, Arrabe, Egipt, Surry,
And all *Europe* halyſly, 540
And for hys worſchip and ualour
Off *Rome* wis fryſt maid Empirour;
Syne in hys capitole wis he,
Throw thaim off hys conſaill privé,
Slayne with puſoune, rycht to the ded; 545
And quhen he ſaw thair wis na rede,
Hys eyn with hys hand cloſit he,
For to dey with mar honeſté.

Ver. 539. *Surry* is *Syria*.

Ver. 545. for *puſoune*, the editions rightly red *bodkins*, that is daggers:

———— might his quietus make
With a bare bodkin.   Shakſp. Hamlet.

Als

Als ARTHUR that, throw chevalry,
Made *Bretane* maistris and lady 550
Off twal kinricks that he wan;
And alsua, as a noble man,
He wan throw bataill *Fraunce* all fre,
And *Lucius Yber* wencusyt he,
That thain off *Rome* wer Empirour; 555
Bot yeit, for all hys gret valour,
MODREYT hys systirs son hym slew.
And gud men als ma then inew,
Throw tresoune, and throw wikkitnes.
The BROICE bers thairoff witnes: 560
Sa fell off this conand making,
For the CUMIN raid to the King

Ver. 549. Our poet here, as usual in his time, blends the most childish fables with history. This account of Arthur is borrowed from Geoffrey of Monmouth; and it appears from Winton that Barbour wrote a book on this subject. Arthur is now known to be a non-existence, being a mere epithet given by the Welsh to Aurelius Ambrosius, *Art-uir,* ' The Great Man.' Gildas was cotemporary with the mock Arthur, 530, but knew nothing of him, tho' in his Epistle *(Gale Script. Angl.)* he mentions five kings of Britain in his time. Nennius, who wrote 858, says nothing of Arthur, the chapter concerning him being an addition after the words, *explicit opus Nennii.* In short, till Geoffrey wrote, 1150, Arthur was unknown. *Arthur's Seat, Arthur's Round Table,* &c. are all names derived from the romances, and tournaments; and unknown, till the thirteenth and fourteenth centuries. Arthur was the Fingal, the Roland, of Wales; nay, of Britain, after Geoffrey's time.

Off *Ingland*, and tald all this cafe;
Bot, I trow, not all as it was.

   Bot the endentur till him gaf he,   565
That foune fchawyt the iniquité:
Quharfor fyne he tholyt ded,
Than he couth fet thairfor nà rede.
Quhen the King faw the endentur,
He wer angry out of mefur,   570
And fwour that he fuld wengeance ta
Off that BRWYSE, that prefumyt fwa
Aganys him to brawle or ryfe,
Or to confpyr on fic a wyfe.
And to Schyr IHON CUMYN faid he   575
That he fuld, for his lawté,
Be rewardyt, and that hely:
And he him thankit humyly.
Than thoucht he to have the leding
Off all *Scotland*, but gane faying,   580
Fra at the BRWYSE to ded war browcht.
Bot oft failyes the ful's thoucht:
And wife menys etling
Cumys not ay to that ending
That thai think it fall cum to,   585
For God wate weill quhat is to do.
Off his etlyng rycht fwa it fell,
As I fall aftirwarts tell,
He tuk hys leve, and hame is went.
And the King a parlyament   590

Gert

Gert fet thaireſtir haſtely;
And thydder fomownys he in hy
The Barownys of his roalté.
And to the Lord the BRWYSE fend he,
Bydding to cum to that gadryng.   595
And he that had na perfawyng
Off the trefoune, na the falſet,
Raid to the King but langir let.
And in *Lundon* him herberyd he,
The fyrſt day of thair aſſembly;   600
Syne on the morn to court he went.
The King fat into parlyament,
And forouch hys cunſaill privé,
The Lord the BRWYSE thair callyt he,
And ſchawyt him the endentur,   605
He wis in full gret aventur
To hym hys lyff; bot God of mycht
Preſerwyt hym till hyer hycht,
That wald not that he fwa war dede.
The King betaucht hym in that ſteid   610
The endentur, the feyle to fe,
And aſkyt gyff it enſelyt he?
He lukyt the feyle ententky,
And anfweryt till him humyly,
And fayd, " How that I fimpell be,   615
" My feyle is not all tyme with me;
" Ye have ane othir it to ber,
" Quarfor gyff that your wills wer,

> Ver. 615. The editions read *throw that*.
> Ver. 617. The fame read *I have*.

" I aſk

"I afk you refpyt for to fe
"This lettir, and thairwith awyfit be,   620
"Till to morn that ye be fet:
"And then, forowtyn langer let,
"This lettir fall I entyr heyr,
"Before all your cunfaill planer;
"And thairtill into borwch draw I   625
"Myn herytage all halily."
The King thoucht he was traift enewch,
Sen he in borwch hys lands drewch:
And let hym with the lettir paffe,
Till entyr it, as forfpokin was.   630

THE END OF BUKE I.

THE

THE
BRUCE.

BUKE II.

ARGUMENT.

ROBERT *flees to Scotland, and kills* CUMIN *at Dumfreis.—*DOUGLAS *meits him neir Lochmaban, and thay becum siker freinds.—*ROBERT *is crounit at Scone—gangs to Perth, and challanges Schir* AYMER DE VALLANGE, *Wardan of Scotland, to battle—is refusit, and ludges in Methven Park—is entrely defait be Schir* AYMER*—retraits to the Grampian Hills—gaes to Aberden, quhar the Quene, and uther ladeis meit him.—Praise of luve and women, ensampiled fra Theban storie.—The Inglis advauncing, the King agane retraits suth-west to the Grampian hills.*

THE
BRUCE.

BUKE II.

THE BRWYSE went till hys innys fwyth,
Bot wyt ye weile he wis full blyth,
That he had gottyn that refpyt.
He callit his marfchall till him tyt,
And bad him luk on all maner;   5
That he ma till hys men gud cher;
For he wald in hys chambre be,
A weill gret quhile in priuaté,
With him a clerk forowtyn ma.
The marfchall till the hall gan ga,   10
And did hys Lordys comanding.
The Lord the BRWYSE, but mar letting,
Gert priuely bryng ftedys twa,
He and the clerk forowtyn ma,
Lap on, forowtyn perfawing,   15
And day and nycht, but foiournying,
Thai raid; quhill, on the fyfte day,
Cumyn till *Louchmaban* ar thai.
Hys brodyr EDUUARD thai thair fand,
That thoucht ferly it tak on hand,

That thai come hame fa priuely:
He tald hys brodyr halyly
How that he thair foucht was,
And how he chapyt wis throw cafe.
Sa fell it in the famyn tyd,   25
That at *Drumfrefe*, rycht thair befide,
Schir IHONE the CUMYN, foiournyng maid,
The BRWYSE lap on, and thydir raid;
And thoucht forowtyn mar letting,
For to qwyt hym hys difcouerying.   30
Thyddir he raid, but langar let,
And with Schyr IHONE the CUMYN met,
In the *Frers*, at the hye awter,
And fchawyt him, with lauchand cher,
The endentur: fyne with a knyff   35
Rycht in that fted hym reft the lyff.
Schyr EDUUARD CUMYN als wis flayn,
And oddirs mony off mekill mayn.

Ver. 26. Dumfries, the celebrated *Caftrum Puellarum*: *Dun, mons, caftellum*; Fre, *puella nobilis*: See the Gloffaries of Wachter, Verelius, &c. Edinburgh is erroneoufly thought the *Caftrum Puellarum*, as it was thought the *Caftra Alata*, tho' the later be Invernefs. Nothing can be more rifible than to fee Irifh etymologifts tell us, that *Dun Edin*, the Irifh name of Edinburgh, implies *Caftra Alata*; but, if they had feen Ptolemy, and known that Invernefs was the *Caftra Alata*, doubtlefs they would have told us that *Invernefs* was Irifh for *Caftra Alata*.

Ver. 33. The church of Minorites, or Gray Friars.

Ver. 37. Sir Robert Cumin, not Sir Edward. But for this, and other particulars concerning this affair, fee Annals of Scotland, I. 291.

Not for this yeit sum men sayis,
That that debat fell othirwayis: 40
Bot quhatsaevyr maid the debate,
Thair throuch he deyt, weill I wat.
He mysdyd that gretly but wer,
That gave na gyrth to the awter.
Thairfor sa hard myscheiff hym fell, 45
That I've herd never in Romanys tell,
Off man sa hard frayit as wis he,
That eftirwart com to sic bounté.

Now agayne to the King ga we;
That on the morn, with hys barné, 50
Sat intill hys parleament;
And eftir the Lord the BRWYSE he sent,
Rycht till his in with knychtys kene.
Quhen he oft tyme had callit been,
And hys men eftir hym askit thai, 55
Thai said that he, sen yhyistirday,
Duelt in hys chambyr ythanly,
With a clark with him evirly.
Than knokyt thai at hys chambyr, thair,
And quhen thai hard nane mak ansuer, 60
Thai brak the dur, bot thai fand nocht,
The quheyir the chambre hale thai foucht.

Ver. 44. *Gyrth* is a sanctuary in Icelandic. To give no gyrth, implies, ' to refuse the place that privilege.'
Ver. 49. Edward of England.
Ver. 58. *Clericus*, a Clergyman? As such alone could write, they were the usual secretaries of the time.

Thai tauld the King than hale the cafe,
And how that he efchepyt was.
He wis of hys efchap fary;   65
And fwair in ire, full ftalwartly,
That he fuld drawyn and hangyt be.
He menaufyt as he thocht, bot he
Thoucht that fuld pafe ane oythir way.
And quhen he, as ye hard me fay,   70
Intill the kyrk Schyr IHONE haid flayn,
Till *Louchmabane* he went againe;
And gert men with hys lettres ryd,
To freynds upon ilk fid,
That come to hym with thair mengye,   75
And hys men als affemblyt he:
And thocht that he wald mak hym king.
Our all the land the word gan fpryng,
That the BRWYSE the CUMYN had flayn;
And amang othyrs lettres ar gayn   80
To the Byfchop of *Androwfe* towne,
That tauld how flayn wis that baroune.
The lettre tauld him all the deid,
And he till hys men gert reid,
And fythyn faid thaim fekyrly,   85
‘ I hop THOMAS prophecy
‘ Off HERSILDOWNE, weryfyd be
‘ In hym; for fwa our Lord help me!

Ver. 86. Thomas Rymour, of Ercildon, a famous poet in his time, 1276, and author of the Romance of Triftram, now unfortunately loft. He was already, 1304, celebrated as a prophet, as Orpheus, Linus, and other early poets.

‘ I haiff

'I haiff gret hop he fall be King,
'And haiff this land all in leding.' 90

JAMES off DOWGLAS that ay quhar
Allways befor the Byschops char,
Had weill hard all the lettre red,
And he tuk alsua full gud hed
To that the Byschop had said. 95
And quhen the burdys doun war laid,
Till chamyr went thai then in hy;
And JAMES of DOWGLAS priuely
Said to the Byschop, 'Schyr, ye se
'How *Inglismen*, throw thair powsté, 100
'Dysheryeys me off my land,
'And men has gert you undirstand,
'Als that the Erle off *Carryk*
'Clamys to govern the kinryk:
'And, for yon man that he has slayn, 105
'All *Inglismen* ar hym agayn,
'And wald disheryse him blythly,
'The quethyr with hym duell wald I.
'Thairfor, Schyr, gyff it war your will,
'I wald tak with hym gud and ill: 110
'Throw hym I trow my land to wyn,
'Magre the CLYFFURD, and hys kyn.'
The Byschop hard, and had pité,
And said, "Swet son, sa God help me!
"I wald blythly that yow war thair, 115
"Bot at I not reprowyt war.

Ver. 96. When the tables were removed.

"On thus maner weile wyrk ye may,
"You fall tak Ferrand my palfray,
"And for thair is na horfe in this land
"Swa fwycht, na yeit fa weill at hand,   120
"Tak hym as off thine awyne he wid,
"As I had gevyn thairto na reid.
"And gyff hys yhemar oucht gruchys,
"Luk that yow tak hym magre his;
"Swa fall I weill affonyeit be.   125
"Mychty God, for hys powſté,
"Graunt, that he that yow paffe to,
"And yow in all tyme fa weill to do,
"'That ye yow fra your fays defend!"
He taucht hym filvir to defpend,   130
And fyne gaiff hym gud day,
And bad him pafe furth on his way,
For he ne wald fpek till he war gane.
The Dowglas than hys way has tane
Rycht to the horfe, as he hym bad;   135
Bot he that hym in yhemfell had,
Than warnyt hym difpitoufly;
Bot he that wreth hym encrely,
Fellyt him with a fuordýs dynt.
And fyne, forowtyn langar ftynt,   140
The horfe he fadylt haftely,
And lap on hym delybritiy,

Ver. 130. Perhaps *raucht*, reached to him, held out to him.
Ver. 139. That is, knocked him down with the back of his fword, or with it undrawn.

And

And paſſyt furth but leve taking.
Der God, that is off Hevyn King!
Sauff him, and ſcheld hym fra hys fayes! 145
All hym alane the way he taes
Towart the towne of *Louchmabane*;
And, a litill fra *Aryk Stane*,
The BRWYSE with a gret rout he met,
That raid to *Scone* for to be ſet 150
In kings ſtole, and to be king.
And quhen DOWGLAS ſaw hys cumyng,
He raid, and hailſyt hym in hy,
And lowtyt hym full curtaſly;
And tauld hym haly all hys ſtate, 155
And quhat he was, and als how gat,
The CLYFFURD held hys heretage:
And that he come to mak homage
Till hym as till hys rychtwiſe King,
And at he boune wer, in all thing, 160

Ver. 150. Scone, the reſidence of our ancient kings. Towns of the ſame name are frequent in Denmark, Norway, and Sweden. In the Saxon dialect of the Gothic, it is *Sheen*, the old name of Richmond. Both words imply *ſhining*, *ſplendid*.

The chief palace of our Pikiſh monarchs was at Forteviot, where Kenneth died 860, according to our old chronicles publiſhed by Innes, in that beſt work on our antiquities, his Critical Eſſay. Forteviot is ſouth of the river Ern, oppoſite to Dupplin. See Fordun, xiii. 23. It is a pity that the ſite and remains of the palace of Forteviot are not inveſtigated. Perhaps curious antiquities may be found buried there. A work on the hiſtory and antiquities of Perthſhire would be very acceptable.

To tak with hym the gud and ill.
And quhen the BRWYSE had herd hys will,
He refawyt him in gret daynté,
And men, and armys, till hym gaff he.
He thoucht weile he fuld be worthy, 165
For all hys eldrs war douchty.
Thus gat maid thai thair aquentance,
That nivir fyne, for na kyn chance,
Depertyt quhill thai lyffand war;
Thair frendfchip woux ay mar and mar; 170
For he ferwyt ay lelely,
And the toddyr full willfully,
That wis bath worthy, wycht, and wyfe,
Rewardyt him weile hys feruice.
The Lord the BRWYSE to *Glafcow* raid, 175
And fend about hym, quhill he haid
Off hys freynds a gret menyhe.
And fyne to *Scone* in hy raid he,
And was maid king but langer let,
And in the kings ftole wer fet: 180

As

Ver. 175. According to Jocelin, in his Life of St. Kentegern, the old name of Glafgow was *Cathures*. In the fame production are feveral curious anecdotes concerning this city. The ftory of the queen of Strath-Clyde's ring, and the falmon, which make part of the arms of Glafgow, fhews that even heraldry is indebted to the Lives of Saints, the chief erudition of the middle ages.

Ver. 180. The famous ftone was fent into England by Edward I. fo that the *king's ftool* here implies a regal chair. The Irifh churchmen, old fathers of our hiftory, (as all our priefts came from Iona, or Icolmkill) fabled that this ftone

came

As in that tyme wis the maner.
Bot off thair noble gret affer,
Thair feruice, na thair roalté,
Ye fall her na thing now for me;
Owtane that he off the barnage   185
That thyddir com, tok homage:
And fyne went our all the land,
Frends, and frendfchip purchefand,
To maynteyin that he had begunyn.
He wyft, or all the land war wounyn,   190
He fuld find full hard barganyng
With hym that wis off *Ingland* King:
For thair wis nane off lyff fa fell,
Sa pantener, na fa cruell.

And quhen to EDUUARD King was tauld, 195
How at the BRWYSE, that wis fa bauld,
Had broucht the CUMYN till ending,
And how he fyne had maid hym King,
Owt off hys wyt he went weill ner;
And callyt till hym Schyr AMER   200

The came from Ireland. But I find no trace of fuch a practice in Ireland; while in Sweden, Denmark, Norway, all the old kings were placed on a ftone, in the midft of a plain, and crowned in view of the people. Such ftones were called *Moraften*. See Olaus Magnus, Loccenius, Mallet, &c. &c.

Robert the Great (if ever king deferved that title) was crowned 27 March 1306.

Ver. 200. Aymer de Vallange, Earl of Pembroke. The reader muft not be furprized at this period to find nobles more frequently defigned by their names than by their titles. Titles had only become hereditary in the eleventh century.

The WALLANG, that was wyſe and wycht,
And off hys hand a worthy knycht,
And bad hym men of armys ta,
And in hy till *Scotland* ga,
And byrn, and ſlay, and raiſe dragoun: 205
And hycht all *Fyfe* in waryſoune,
Till hym that mycht othir ta or ſla
ROBERT the BRWYSE, that was his fa.
Schyr AMER did as he hym bad,
Gret chewalry with hym he had; 210
With hym was PHILIP the MOWBRAY,
And INGRAM the UMFRAWELL perſay,
That was bath wyſe and awerty,
And full of gret chewalry;
And off *Scotland* the maiſt party 215
Thai had intill thair cumpany.
For yheit then mekill off the land
Was intill *Ingliſmenys* hand.
Till *Perth* then went thai in a rout,
That then was wallyt all about 220
With

century. The firſt *Earls* were merely ſheriffs of counties: and the popular mouth was not yet accuſtomed to the innovation.

Ver. 205. I know not the meaning of *dragoun*: the editions ſeem rightly to read *dungeoun*, that is, *keeps* or forts to bridle the rebels.

Ver. 211. Of the Moubrays, a Norman race, there were powerful families both in England and Scotland. The name is ſtill common in the later country.

Ver. 212. Inghiram de Umfraville.

Ver. 219. A town noted in the old annals of war, and
now

With feile towrs, rycht hy battulyt,
To defend gyff it wer affaylit.
Thairin dwellyt Schyr AMERY,
With all hys gret chewalry;
The King ROBERT wyft he wer thair,   225
And quhat kyn chyftanys with him war,
And affemblyt all hys mengye;
He had feyle off full gret bounté,
Bot thair fayis wer mar than thai,
Be fifteen hundred, as I've hard fay.   230
The quhere he had thair, at that ned,
Full feill that war douchty of deid;
And barownys that war bauld as bar.
Twa Erles alfua with hym war,
Off LENYVAX and ATHOLL war thai;   235
EDUUARD the BRWYSE was thair alfa,

THOMAS now for the arts of peace. It feems to have been the *Victoria* of the Romans, according to Ptolemy's map. It is needlefs to inform the reader, that the *Bertha* of Hector Boyce never exifted, but in that forger's brain. If Mr. Pennant had feen Innes's Effay, or at all known the character of Hector, he would not have ftained his amiable pages with many an error from that fabulift.

Ver. 235—240. Thefe heroic friends of Bruce are Malcom, fifth Earl of *Lenyvax*, or Lennox, now part of Dunbartonfhire. John of Strathbogie, tenth Earl of Athol, a country noted as a grand divifion of Scotland from early times: (*Defcr. Albaniæ apud Innes*). Edward the king's brother. Thomas Randel, afterward Earl of Moray. Hew Hay, brother of Gilbert Hay, of Errol; a family palpably of Norman extract, *de la Haye*, ' of the hedge,' in fpite of Boyce's fables concerning it, and Douglas. Such families
ftand

THOMAS RANDELL, and HEW DE LE HAY,
And Schyr DAUID the BERCLAY,
FRESALE, SUMMIRWILE, and INCHMERTYN;
IAMES of DOWGLAS thair wis fyne,   240
That yheyet than wis bot litill of mycht:
And othir fele folk forfye in fycht,
Bot I cannot tell quhat thai hycht.
Thoucht thai war quheyn thai war worthy,
And full of gret chewalry.   245
And in bataill, in gud aray,
Befor Saint *Ihonyftoun* com thai,
And bad Schyr AMERY ifch to fycht;
And he, that in the mekill mycht
Traiftyt off thaim that wis hym by,   250
Bad hys men arme thaim haftily.
Bot Schyr INGRAM THE UMFRAWILL
Thoucht it war all to gret perill
In playne bataill to thaim to ga,
Or quhill thai war arrayit fa.   255
And till Schyr AMER faid he,
' Schyr, giff that ye will trow to me,
' Ye fall not ifche thaim till affaile,
' Till thai ar purwayt in bataill;

ftand in no need of fictions to adorn them. David Barclay, of Cairns in Fife. Alexander Frefal, (or Frafer in modern fpelling,) brother of Simon Frafer, of Oliver-caftle. Walter de Somerville, of Linton and Carnwath. David of Inchmartin. James Baron Douglas. See *Ann. of Scotl.* II. 2.

Ver. 247. Saint John's town is well known to be another name for Perth.

' For

' For thair ledar is wycht and wyſe, 260
' And off hys hand a noble knycht is;
' And he has in hys cumpany
' Mony a gud man, and worthy,
' That ſall be hard for till aſſay,
' Till thai ar in ſa gud aray. 265
' For it ſuld be full mekill mycht,
' That now ſuld put thaim to the flycht:
' For quhen folk ar weill arayit,
' And for the bataill weill purwait,
' With this that thai all gud men be, 270
' Thai ſall fer mar be awiſé,
' And weill mar for to dreid, than thai
' War ſet ſum dele out off aray.
' Thairfor ye mayſe ſay thaim till
' That thai may this nycht, and thai will, 275
' Gang herbery thaim, and ſlep and reſt;
' And at to morn but langar left
' Ye ſall iſch furth to the bataill,
' And fecht with thaim, but gyff thai faile.
' Sa till thair herbery went ſall thai, 280
' And ſum ſall went to the forray,
' And thai that duellis at the logyng,
' Sen thai cum owt off trewelling,
' Sall in ſchort tyme unarmyt be.
' Then on owr beſt maner may we, 285
' With all owr fayr chewalry,
' Ryd towart thaim rycht hardyly;
' And thai that wenys to reſt all nycht
' Quhen thai ſe us arayit to fycht,

' Cumand

' Cumand on thaim fa fudanly, 290
' Thai fall affiriyit gretumly.
' And or thai cumyn in bataill be,
' We fall fpeid us fwa gat that we
' Sall be all redy till affembill.
' Sum man for eryneft will trymbill, 295
' Quhen he affayit is fudanly,
' That with awifement is douchty.'

As he awyfit now have thai done;
And till thaim utouth fend thai fone,
And bad thaim herbery thaim that nycht, 300
And on the morn cum to the fycht.
Quhen thai faw thai mycht no mar,
Towart *Meffayn* then gan thai far;
And in the woud thaim logyt thai:
The thrid pert went to the forray; 305
And the lave fone unarmyt war,
And fkalyt to loge thaim her and ther.

Schyr AMER then, but mar abaid,
With all the folk he with him haid,
Ifchyt in forcely to the fycht, 310
And raid intill a randoun rycht,

Ver. 304. *Meffayn*, the vulgar pronunciation of *Methven*. The *th*, fo familiar to the Goths, Saxons, Icelanders, Greeks, as to form but one letter, is apt to be corrupted by fome nations into *d*. But the Ruffians corrupt it to *f*, faying *Feodor* for *Theodor*; as the Englifh change *gh* to *f*, in *laugh*. Methven is a village between Tibber-moor and Almond-river, not far from Perth, on the north-weft.

The

The ſtrawcht way towart *Meffen.*
The KING, that wis unarmyt then,
Saw thaim cum ſwa enforcely,
Then till hys men gan hely cry,   315
" Till armys ſwyth, and makys you yar!
" Her at our hand our ſayis ar!"
And thai did ſwa in full gret hy;
And on thair horſe lap haſtily.
The KING diſplayit hys baner,   320
Quhen that hys folk aſſemblyt wer,
And ſaid, " Lordings, now may ye ſe
" That yone folk all, throw ſutelté,
" Schapis thaim to do with ſlycht,
" That at thai drede to do with mycht.   325
" Now I perſawe he that will trow
" His fa, it fall hym ſum tyme row.
" And noucht for this, thoucht thai be fele,
" God may rycht weill our werds dele;

Ver. 320. The banner of Scotland, as may be ſuppoſed; the lion with a treſſure of ſpear-heads, facetiouſly called *fleurs de lis,* tho' uſed by William the Lion, A. D. 1165, as appears from his ſeal, while the *fleur de lis* is only known in the time of Philip the Hardy, king of France, A. D. 1270, and was taken from the gold coins of Florence, with that flower; in imitation of which *florins* were coined in France, after a long ceſſation of gold coinage. See *Le Blanc, Monnoyes de France,* &c. It appears, from Sir George Mackenzie's book on heraldry, that Bruce's own arms were an *Orle,* ſo called from *Orula,* ' a little border;' and is a treſſure within a ſhield, the field appearing in the middle.

Ver. 322. This ſpeech is not devoid of ſoldierly eloquence.

" For

"For multitud mayſe na victory; 330
"As men has red in mony ſtory,
"That few folk has oft wencuſyt ma.
"Trow we that we ſall do rycht ſua.
"Ye are ilkan wycht and worthy,
"And full of gret chewalry; 335
"And wate rycht weill quhat honour is.
"Wyrk yhe then apon ſwylk wyſe,
"That your honour be ſawyt ay.
"And a thing will I to you ſay,
"That he that deis for hys cuntré 340
"Sall herbryit intill hewyn be."

Quhen this wis ſaid thai ſaw cumand
Thair fayis ridand, ner at the hand,
Arayit rycht awiſely,
Willfull to do chewalry. 345
On aythir ſyd thus war thai yhar,
And till aſſemble all redy war.
Thai ſtrawcht thair ſpers, on aythir ſyd,
And ſwa ruydly gan ſamyn ryd,
That ſpers at ſo fruſchyt war, 350
And feyle men dede, and woundyt ſar,
The blud owt at thair byrnys breſt.
For the beſt, and the worthieſt,
That wilfull war to wyn honour,
Plungyt in the ſtalwart ſtour, 355
And routs ruyd about thaim dang.
Men mycht haiff ſeyn into that thrang

Knychts that wycht and hardy war,
Undyr horfe feyt defpulyt thair;
Sum woundyt, and fum all ded,   360
The grefe woux off the blud all rede.
And thai that held on horfe in hy
Swappyt owt fwerds fturdyly;
And fwa fell ftrakys gave and tuk,
That all the reuk about thaim quouk.   365
The BRUYSE's folk full hardely
Schawyt thair gret chewalry:
And he hymfelff, atour the lave,
Sa hard and fa hewy dints gave,
That quhar he come thai maid hym way.   370
Hys folk thaim put in hard affay,
To ftynt thair fais mekill mycht,
That then fo fayr had off the fycht,
That thai wan feild ay mar and mar:
The KINGS fmall folk ner wencufyt ar.   375
And quhen the KING hys folk has fene
Begyn to faile, for proper tene,
Hys affenyhe gan he cry,
And in the ftour fa hardyly

Ver. 378. The *enfenyie*, or *affenyie*, is the word of war. It was generally the name of the leader, as *A Bruce! A Bruce! Douglas!* &c. Sometimes that of the chief's refidence, or of a noted victory gained by his anceftors. The grand word of France, when the *oriflamme*, or royal banner, was difplayed, was *Saint Dennis!* of England, *Saint George!* I know not if *Saint Andrew* was ever ufed in Scotland.

VOL. I.   E   He

He ruſchyt, that all the ſemble ſchuk: 380
He all till hewyt that he ourtuk;
And dang on thaim quhill he mycht drey.
And till hys folk he cryt hey,
" On thaim! On thaim! Thai feble faſt!
" This bargane nevir may langar laſt!" 385
And with that word ſa willfully
He dang on, and ſa hardely,
That quha had ſene hym in that fycht
Suld hald hym for a douchty knycht.
Bot thoucht he wis ſtout and hardy, 390
And othyrs als off hys cumpany,
Thair mycht na worſchip thair awailye;
For thair ſmall folk begouth to failye,
And fled all ſkalyt her and thar.
Bot the gude at enchauſyt war, 395
Off ire abide, and held the ſtour
To conquyr thaim endles honour.

And quhen Schyr AMER has ſene
The ſmall folk fle all bedene;
And ſa few abid to fycht; 400
He releyt to hym mony a knycht,
And in the ſtour ſa hardyly,
He ruſchyt with hys chewalry,

Ver. 384. The king, as appears from the ſequel, only uſes theſe words to encourage his men, for the foe was far from drooping.

That

That he ruſchyt his fayis ilkane.
Schyr THOMAS RANDELL thair wis tane, 405
That then wis a young bacheler;
And Schyr ALEXANDIR FRASEYR;
And Schyr DAVID the BREKLAY,
INCHMERTYNE, and HEW DE LE HAY,
And SOMIRWEIL, and othyr ma; 410
And the KING hymſelff alſua,
Was ſet untill full hard aſſay,
Throw Schyr PHILIP the MOWBRAY,
That raid till hym full hardyly,
And hynt hys rengye, and ſyne gane cry, 415
" Help! help! I have the new maid King!"
With that come gyrdand, in a lyng,
CRYSTALL of SEYTOUN, quhen he ſwa
Saw the KING ſeſyt with hys fa,
And to PHILIP ſic rout he raucht, 420
That thocht he wis off mekill maucht,
He gert hym galay diſyly,
And haid till erd gaue fullyly.
Ne war he hynt hym by hys ſted
Then off hys hand the brydill yhed; 425

Ver. 405. Randel, to ſecure his life, ' turned Engliſh-man,' as the phraſe of the times was; that is, he for a time acceded to the Engliſh intereſt. But he ſoon after returned to his duty, as the ſequel will ſhew.

Ver. 418. Chriſtopher Seton, of Seton, anceſtor of the Duke of Gordon, Earl of Winton, Earl of Dunfermlin, and Vicount Kingſton. *Annals*, II. 2.

And the KING hys eſſenye gan cry,
Releyt hys men that war hym by,
That war ſa few that thai na mycht
Endur the forſe mar off the fycht.
Thai prikyt then out off the preſe;   430
And the KING that angry was,
For he hys men ſaw fle hym fra,
Said then, "Lordings, ſen it is ſwa
"That wre runnys again us her,
"Gud is we paſs off ther daunger,   435
"Till God us ſend eftſone hys grace;
"And yeyt man fall, giff thai will chace,
"Quyt thaim combat ſum dele we ſall."
To this word thai aſſentyt all,
And fra thaim walopyt owyr mar;   440
Thair fayis alſua wery war,
That off thaim all thai chaſeyt nane:
Bot with priſoners, that thai had tane,
Rycht to the towne thai held thair way,
Rycht glaid and joyfull off thair pray. 445

That nycht thai lay all in the toun,
Ther was nane off ſa gret renoun,

Ver. 426. The king's preſence of mind and courage are here very conſpicuous. Inſtead of concealing himſelf, or deſponding, he proclaims who he is; and endeavours to rally and protect his ſcattered band.

Ver. 434. Editions read *weir*; perhaps *ure*.

Na yeit ſa hardy off thaim all,
That durſt herbery without the wall.
Sa dred thai ſar the gayne cumyng 450
Off Schyr ROBERT, the douchty King.
And to the King off *Ingland* ſone,
Thai wrate haly as thai haid done;
And he wis blyth off that tything,
And for diſpyte bad draw and hing 455
All the priſoners, thoucht thai war ma.
Bot Schyr AMER did not ſwa;
To ſum bath land and lyff gaiff he,
To leve the BRWYSE ſewté,
And ſerve the King off *Ingland*, 460
And off hym for to hald the land:
And werray the BRWYSE as thair ſa.
THOMAS RANDELL was ane off tha,
That for hys lyff become thair man.
Off othyrs, that war takyn than, 465
Sum thai ranſowmyt, ſum thai ſlew,
And ſum thai hangyt, and ſum thai drew.

In this maner ROBERT was
The BRWYSE, that mekill murning mayſe
For hys men that war ſlayne and tane. 470
And he was als ſa will off wane,
That he trowyt in nane ſekyrly,
Owtane thaim off hys cumpany;

Ver. 463. Randel, as after ſeen, became very faithful to his new friends, to whom gratitude attached him.

That war fa few that thai mycht be
Five hunder ner off all mengye. 475
Hys brodyr alwayis was hym by,
Schyr EDUUARD, that was fa hardy;
And with hym was a bauld baroun,
Schyr WILYAM THE BOROUNDOUN;
The ERLE of ATHOLE als was thair. 480
Bot ay fyn thai difcomfyt war,
The ERLE off the LENEUAX wis away,
And was put to full hard affay,
Or he met with the KING agayn:
Bot allways, as a man of mayn, 485
He maynteinyt him full manfully.
The KING had in hys cumpany
JAMES alfua of DOWGLAS,
That wycht, wyfe, and worthy was;
Schyr GILBERT DE LE HAY alfua; 490
Schyr NELE CAMBELL, and othyrs ma,
That I thair namys can not fay,
As utelauys went mony day;

Ver. 479. This name of Borundon does not, I believe, occur in any other monuments of our hiftory. Perhaps he was a foreigner, a Fleming.

Ver. 491. Niel Campbell, predeceffor of the noble houfe of Argyle. This name, Niel, is latinized *Nigellus* by the barbarous writers of the time; but is really the Scandinavian *Nial*, which paffed to Ireland and Scotland with the Danes. The great houfe of Campbell is of Norman extract: and the highland fenachies, fo utterly fabulous in moft other genealogies, allow this.

Dreand

Dreand in the *Month* thair payne;
Eyte flefch, and drank water fyne.   495
He durft not to the planys ga,
For all the cummownys went hym fra;
That for thair liff war full fayn
To pafs to the *Inglis* pes agayn:
Sa fayrs ay cummounly;   500
In cummownys may nane affy:
Bot he that may thair warrand be.
Sa fur thai then with hym, for he
Thaim fra thair fais mycht nocht warrand:
Thai turnyt to the tothyr hand.   505
Bot threldome, that men gert thaim fele,
Gert thaim ay yarne that he fur wele.

   Thus in the hyllis levyt he,
Till the maift pert off hys menye
Wer rewyn, and rent, na fchoyne thai had,   510
Bot as thai thaim off hydys mad.

   Ver. 494. Editions read,
        Dreeing in the mountains payne.
The *Month*, or *Mounth*, is a term in our old writers for two great chains of mountains; one in Caithnefs, *Mons Mound dividit Cathanefiam per medium*: Defcr. Albaniæ, apud Innes, fcript. cir. 1180: the other the famous Grampian chain, reaching from the top of Lochlomond into Aberdeenfhire. The later is here meant; the *Month* is the *Mons Grampius* of Tacitus. The name feems from *Gram*, Icelandic, 'a warrior;' hence all warlike works are called *Grams Dikes*, from that twenty miles north of London, even to the north of Scotland.

Thairfor thai went till *Abyrdeyne*,
Quhair NELE the BRWYSE come, and the QUEYN,
And othyr ladyis fayr, and farand,
Ilkane for luff off thair hufband; 515
That for leyle luff, and loawté,
Wald pertenerys off thair paynys be.
Thai chefyt tyttar with thaim to ta
Angyr, and payn; na be thaim fra.
For luff is off fa mekill mycht, 520
That it all paynys maks licht.
And mony tyme mafe tender wycht
Of fwilk ftrenthtes, and fwilk mycht,
That thai may mekill paynys endur,
And forfakis nane auentur 525
That euer may fall, withthy that thai
Thairthrow fuccur thair luffys may.

Men redys when *Thebes* wis tane,
And King ARISTAS men war flane,

Ver. 512. Aberdeen, the *Divana* of Ptolemy, the *Apurden* of Icelandic writers. Scotifh names in *Aber* are ridiculoufly fuppofed Welch; but they abound in Germany, and there is an *Aberden* in the duchy of Bremen, *Aberburg* in Livonia, &c. &c. The word Aber, or Ober, in German, implies *over, beyond, upon*. See Wachter.

Ver. 513. Niel de Bruce, fecond brother to the King. The Queen fo known for her misfortunes was Elizabeth, daughter of Aymer de Burgh, Earl of Ulfter, fecond wife of King Robert. His firft was Ifabella, daughter of Donald, Earl of Mar. *Annals.*—King Robert at this time was aged thirty-two, being born 11 July 1274.

Ver. 528. See this ftory in the laft book of the Thebais of Statius.

That

That assailyt the cité,   530
That the women off hys cuntré
Come for to fech hym hame agayne,
Quhen thai hard all hys folk was slayne.
Quhar the King CAMPANEUS,
Throw the help of MENESTEUS,   535
That come per case rydand tharby,
With three hunder in cumpany,
That throw the King's prayer assailyt,
That yeit to tak the toune had failyeit.
Then war the wiffys thyrland the wall   540
With pikks, quhar the assailyers all
Entryt, and dystroyit the tour,
And slew the peipill but retour.
Syn quhen the Duk hys way wis gayne;
And all the Kings men war slayne;   545
The wiffs had him till hys cuntré,
Quhar was na man leiffand bot he.

In women mekill cumfort lyis;
And gret solace on mony wife.
Sa fell yt her for thair cumyng   550
Reiosyt rycht gretumly the KING;
The quheyr ilk nycht hymsel wys wouk,
And hys rest upon dayis touk.

A gud quhile ther he soiournyt then,
And esyt wondir weill hys men;   555
Till that the *Inglis* men herd say
That he thair with hys mengye lay,

All

All at efe. And fykerly
Affemblyt thai thair oft in hy;
And ther him trowit to furprife.   565
Bot he, that in hys deid wis wyfe,
Wyft thai affemblyt war, and quhar;
And wyft that thai fa mony war,
That he mycht not agayne thaim fycht.
Hys men on hy he gert be dycht,   565
And bufkyt, off the toune to ryd:
The ladyis raid rycht by hys fyd.
Than to the hill thai raid thar way,
Quhar gret defaut of mete had thai.
Bot worthy JAMES off DOWGLAS,   570
Ay trewailland and befy was,
For to purches the ladyis mete;
And it on mony wife wald get.
For quhile he venefoun thaim brocht:
And with hys hands quhiles he wrocht   575
Gynnys, to tak gedds and falmonys,
Trowts, elys, and als menownys.
And quhill thai went to the forray;
And fwa thair purchefyng maid thai:
Ilk man treweillyt for to get   580
And pourchefs thaim that thai mycht ete.
Bot off all that evir thai war,
Thar wis not ane amang thaim thar,

Ver. 576. *Gedds*, a fmall fifh rather larger than minnons; *elys*, eels; *menownys*, a fmall frefh-water fifh, called in Scotland *minnons*, in England *menons*.

That

That to the Ladyis profyt was
Mar than Jamys off Dowglas.   585
And the King oft cumfort was,
Throw hys wyt, and hys befynes.
On this maner thaim gouernyt thai
Till thai come to the hed of *Tay.*

THE END OF BUKE II.

THE
BRUCE

BUKE III.

ARGUMENT.

The King cumyng be Loch Tay to Lorn, the Lord of LORN, *nevew of* CUMIN, *assembles the men of Lorn and Argyle to assail him.* — *The King retraits* — *but kills thrie faes quha attack him. To solace his men, he tells the storie of Rome and* HANNIBAL. — *The Erle of* ATHOLE *gangs with the Quene and Ladeis to Kildrumy.* — *The King sayls ouir Loch Lomond* — *meits his frend the Erle of* LEVENAX — *sayls be the ile of Bute to Kintyre, and is weil recevit be* ANGUS *of Ilay* — *proceids to the ile of Rachrin, quhar he remanes hale wyntir.*

THE BRUCE.

BUKE III.

THE Lord of LORN wenyt tharby,
That wis capitale ennymy
To the KING, for hys Emy's fak,
IOHN COMYN. And thocht for to tak
Wengeance, upon cruell maner, 5
Quhen he the KING wyft wis fa ner.

Ver. 1. 'Alexander of Argyle, Lord of Lorn, had married the aunt of Comyn,' fays Sir D. Dalrymple, *Annals*, II. 6. for this Fordun, XII. 2. is quoted. But I cannot find the paffage; and it is clear from Barbour, that Alexander, Lord of Argyle, was the father of John, Lord of Lorn, here mentioned. See Book X. Thefe Lords of Argyle, Lorn, Rofs, and the Iles, were all Norwegians, as are the chief families in thefe countries at this day: nor can they be regarded as really fubject to Scotland, till the fixteenth century. Rymer, in his Fœdera, VIII. 415, 527, has publifhed an alliance between Henry IV. and the Lord of the Iles, 1408. The great Mac Donalds were of direct Norwegian race; and the *Mac* is by no means a mark of the contrary, being an ufual abbreviation among their fubjects for *fon of*; and doubtful if not from the Norwegian *Magd, filius vel filia*. Our *Macbeth* is called *Magbeth* by Icelandic writers.

He

He assemblyt hys men in hy,
And had intill hys cumpany
The barownys off *Argyle* alsua;
Thai war a thousand weill or ma:	10
And come for to supprise the KING,
That weill wis war off thair cumyng.
Bot all to few with him he had,
The quheyir he bauldly thaim abaid;
And weill oft, at thair fryst metyng,	15
War layd at erd, but recoveryng:
The KINGS folk full weill thaim bar,
And slew, and fellyt, and woundyt sar.
Bot the folk off the tothyr party
Fawcht with axys sa fellyly,	20
For thai on fute war evir ilk ane,
That that feile off the horss has slayne;
And till sum gaiff thai wounds wid.
JAMES off DOWGLAS was hurt that tyd;
And als Schyr GILBERT DE LE HAY.	25
The KING hys men saw in affray,
And hys ensonye can he cry;
And amang thaim rycht hardyly
He raid, that he thaim ruschyt all,
And sele of thaim thar gert he fall.	30
Bot quhen he saw thai war sa feill,
And saw thaim swa gret dynts deill,

Ver. 20. The pol-ax, an old Norwegian weapon. See Bartholin, &c. The Lochaber ax is the *lang-bard* used in war, as the *bal-bard* in the halls of princes.

He dred to tyne hys folk, for thy
Hys men till hym he gan rely,
And said, ' Lordyngs, foly it war
' Tyll us for till assembill mar,
' For thai fele off our horse has slayn;
' And gyff ye fecht with thaim agayn
' We fall tyne off our small mengye,
' And ourselffs fall in perill be.
' Tharfor me thynk maist awenand
' To withdraw us, us defendand,
' Till we come out off thair danger,
' For our strenth at our hand is ner.'

Than thai withdrew thaim halely;
Bot that wis not full cowartly,
For samyn intill a sop held thai,
And the King him abandonyt ay
To defend behind hys mengye.
And throw hys worschip sa wroucht he,
That he reskewyt all the flears,
And styntyt swa-gat the chassars,
That nane durst owt off bataill chase,
For alwayis at thair hand he was.
Sa weile defendyt he hys men,
That quhasaevir had seyne hym then
Prowe sa worthely wasselage,
And turn sa oft sythis the wisage,
He suld say he awcht weill to be
A King of a gret rowaté.

VOL. I.   F   Quhen

Quhen that the Lord of LORN faw
Hys men ftand off hym ane fik aw,
That thai durft not folow the chafs,
Rycht angry in hys hart he was;
And for wondyr that he fuld fwa   65
Stot thaim, hym ane but ma,
He faid, " Methink, MARTHOKYS fon,
" Rycht as GOLMAKMORN was wone
" To haiff fra hym all hys mengye:
" Rycht fwa all hys fra us has he."   70

He fet enfample thus mydlike,
The quheyir he mycht, mar manerlik,

Lyknyt

Ver. 67. This curious paffage in the edition of Glafgow, 1737, 12mo, p. 35, ftands thus:
   He faid, Methink Martheokes fon,
   Right as Gowmakmorn was won
   To have from Fyngal his menzie:
   Right fo from us all his hes he.

It appears to me that the tranfcriber of this MS. not knowing *Fyngal*, has by miftake put *hym all*; for the paffage is not fenfe as it ftands in the text. Martheok's fon feems the perfon to whom Lorn fpeaks. Gol Mak Morn is Gaul fon of Morni, fo famous in Irifh tradition.

The paffage alfo ftands as in this note in the Edinburgh edition, 1616, 8vo, the earlieft known, and in all the others which the editor has feen.

Ver. 71. Barbour having no prophetic view of Offian, and little fufpecting that Scotland would in the eighteenth century produce a Geoffrey of Monmouth, has here fpoken with great contempt of the comparifon ufed by Lorn.

Mr. Pennant, III. 14, mentions, that a brotch which

Bruce

Lyknyt hym to GAUDIFER DE LARYSS,
Quhen that the mychty Duk BETYSS
Assailyeit in *Gadyrrs* the forrayours.   75
And quhen the King thaim maid recours,
Duk BETYSS tuk on hym the flycht,
That wald ne mar abid to fycht.
Bot gud GAUDIFER the worthy
Abandonyt hym so worthyly,   80
For hys reskew all the fleiers,
And for to stonay the chassers,
That ALEXANDER to erth he bar;
And alsua did he THOLIMAR,
And gud CONEUS alsua,   85
DANKLINE alsua, and othyr ma.
Bot at the last thar slayne he wis:
In that failyeit the liklynes.

   For the KING, full chewalrusly,
Defendyt all hys cumpany,   90
And wis set in full gret danger;
And yeit eschapyt haile and fer.

   For twa broythirs wer in that land,
That war the hardiest off hand

Bruce lost on this occasion was long preserved in the Mac Dougal family. A watch, said to have belonged to Robert Bruce, is now in the King's possession. See an account of it in the Archæologia. From the best authority, that of a Professor in the University of Glasgow, the public is informed that this watch was made by a pedlar and engraver of Glasgow, about fifteen years ago.

That war intill all that cuntré: 95
And thai hav fworn, iff thai mycht fe
The BRWYSE, quhar thai mycht hym ourta,
That thai fuld dey, or then hym fla.
Thair furname was *Makyne Droffer*;
That is alfo mekill to fay her 100
As the *Durwarth fonnys* perfay.
Off thair cowyne the thrid had thai;
That wis rycht ftout, ill, and feloun.
Quhen thai the KING of gret renoun
Saw fua behind hys mengie rid, 105
And faw hym torne fa mony tid,
Thai abaid till that he was
Entryt in ane narrow place,
Betwyx a louch fyd and a bra;
That wis fa ftract, I underta, 110
That he mycht not weill turn hys fted.
Than with a will till hym thai yede;
And ane hym by the bridill hynt:
Bot he raucht till hym fic a dynt,
That arme and fchuldyr flaw hym fra. 115
With that ane oythir gan hym ta
By the lege, and hys hand gan fchute
Betwix the fterap, and hys fute:
And quhen the KING feld thar hys hand,
In hys fterapys ftythly gan he ftand, 120
And ftrak with fpurs the ftede in hy,
And he lanfyt furth delyvirly.

Ver. 109. *Louch*, the old Saxon *luh*, a lake. See Lye's
Dict. Sax. Goth. Hence our *loch*.

Sa

Sa that the tothyr failyeit fete,
And not forthy his hand wis yeit
Undyr the sterap, magre his. 125
The thrid with full gret hy with this
Rycht till the bra syd he yeid,
And stert behynd hym on hys sted:
The KING wis then in full gret press,
The quheythir he thocht as he that wes 130
In all hys dedys awise,
To doe ane owtrageouss bounté.
And syne hym that behynd hym wass,
All magre hys will hym gan he rass
Fra behynd hym, thoch he had sworn, 135
He laid hym ewyn hym beforn.
Syne with the suerd sik dynt hym gave,
That he the heid till the harnys clave:
He rouschit doun off blud all rede,
As he that stound feld off dede. 140
And then the KING in full gret hy,
Strak at the toythir wigorusly,
That he eftir hys sterap drew,
That at the fyrst strak he hym slew.
On this wiss hym delyverit he 145
Off all the felloun fayis thre,

Qhen

Ver. 146. It must be remarked, that Barbour here makes Robert kill *three* men; other *three*, book v.; other *three*, book vij.; *five*, book vi.; *fourteen*, ibid. There is a shocking improbability in these events: Alfred, and *Henri Quatre*, never

Qhen thai off *Lorne* has fene the KING
Set in hymfelff fa gret helping,
And defendyt hym fa manlely;
Wis nane amang thaim fa hardy 150
That durft affailye hym mar in fycht:
Sa dred thai for hys mekill mycht.
There was a Baroun MAKNAUCHTAN,
That in hys hart gret kep has tane
To the KINGS chewalry, 155
And prefyt hym in hert gretly.
And to the Lord off LORNE faid he,
' Sekyrly now may ye fe
' Betane the ftarkeft pundelayn,
' That ewyr your lyff tyme ye faw tane. 160
' For yone knycht, throw hys douchty deid,
' And throw hys outrageous manheid,
' Has fellyt intill litill tyd
' Thre men of mekill mycht and prid:
' And ftonayit all owr mengye fa, 165
' That eftir hym dar na man ga;
' And tournys fa mony tyme hys ftede,
' That femys off us he had na dred.'

never met with fuch. The repetition of *three* would be naufeous in a romance, in hiftory it is impoffible and falfe. If the reader looks on all thefe tales as fabulous, he has reafon on his fide.

Ver. 153. The Mac Naughtans were powerful in Cowal.
Ver. 159, 160. Editions read,
   Betane the ftarkeft pondelayne
   That in your lifetime ye faw ane.
            Then

Then gane the Lord of LORNE fay,
" It femys it likis the perfay, 170
" That he flayis yon gat our mengye."
' Schyr,' faid he, ' fa our Lord me fe !
' To fauff your prefence it not fwa,
' Bot quhythir he be freynd or fa,
' That wynnys pryfs off chewalry, 175
' Men fuld fpek tharoff lelyly.
' And fekyrly, in all my tyme,
' Ife hard nevir, in fang na ryme,
' Tell off a man that fwa fmertly
' Efchewyt fwa gret chewalry.' 180

 Sic fpeking off the KING thai maid:
And he eftyr hys mengye raid;
And intill faufté thaim led,
Quhar he hys fayis na thing dred.
And thai off *Lorne* agayn ar gayn, 185
Menand the fcaith that thai haiff tayn.

 The KING that nycht hys wachis fet,
And gert ordayne that thai mycht et;
And bad conford to thaim tak,
And at thair mychts mery mak. 190
' For difconford,' as then faid he,
' Is the werft thing that may be.
' For throw mekill difconforting
' Men fallis oft into difparyng.
' And fra a man difparyt be, 195
' Then trowly utterly wencufyt is he.

' And

‘ And fra the hart be difcumfyt,
‘ The body is not worth a mit.
‘ Tharfor,’ he faid, ‘ atour all thing,
‘ Kepys yow fra difparyng :   200
‘ And thynk thouch we now harmys fele,
‘ That God may yeit releve us weill.
‘ Men redys off mony men that war
‘ Fer hardar ftad then we yhet ar,
‘ And fyne our Lord fic grace thaim lent,   205
‘ That thai come weill till thair intent.

‘ For *Rome* quhiles fa hard was ftad,
‘ Quhen HANNIBALL thaim wencufyt had,
‘ That off ryngs with rich ftaynys,
‘ That war off knychts fyngyrs taneys,   210
‘ He fend thre bollis to *Cartage*.
‘ And fyne to *Rome* tuk hys woage,
‘ Thar to diftroye the cité all ;
‘ And thai within, bath gret and fmall,
‘ Had fled, quhen thai faw hys cumyng,   215
‘ Had not bene SCIPIO the king ;
‘ That or thai fled wald thaim haiff flayn,
‘ And fwa gat turnyt he thaim agayn.
‘ Syne for to defend the cité,
‘ Bath ferwands and threllis mad he fre ;   220
‘ And maid thaim knychts evir ilkane.
‘ And fyne has off the templis tane

Ver. 220. A *threll* is a flave. *Thral, fervus*, Icelandic. It is a common term in that curious work *Iflands Landnamabok*, Hafn. 1774, 4to.

‘ The

‘ The armys, that thair eldrys bar,
‘ In name of wictory offerayt thar.
‘ And quhen thai armyt war, and dycht, 225
‘ That ftalwart karlis war and wycht,
‘ And faw that thai war fre alfua,
‘ Thaim thocht that thai had leuir ta
‘ The dede, na lat the toune be tane.
‘ And with comowne affent, as ane, 230
‘ Thai ifchyt off the toune to fycht,
‘ Quhar HANYBALL hȳs mekill mycht
‘ Aganys thaim arayit was.
‘ Bot, throw mycht of Godds grace,
‘ It ranyt fa hard, and hewyly, 235
‘ That thar wis nane fa hardy
‘ That durft into that place abid;
‘ Bot fped thaim intill hy to rid:
‘ The ta pairt to thair parlyownys,
‘ The tothyr pairt went in the toune is. 240
‘ The rayne thus lettyt the fechtyn:
‘ Sa did it twifs thareftir fyne.
‘ Quhen HANIBALL faw this ferly,
‘ With all hys gret chewalry,
‘ He left the toune, and held hys way; 245
‘ And fyne wis put to fik affay,
‘ Throw the power off that cité,
‘ That hys lyff and hys land tynt he.

‘ Be thȳr quheyne, that fo worthily
‘ Wane fic a king, and fa mychty, 250
‘ Ye

' Ye may weill enſampill ſe,
' That na man ſuld diſparyt be:
' Na lat hys hart be wencuſyt all,
' For na myſcheiff that euir may fall.
' For nane wate, in how litill ſpace,   255
' That God umquhile will ſend grace.
' Had thai fled, and thair wayis gane,
' Thair fayis ſwith the toune had tane.
' Tharfor men that werrayand war,
' Suld ſet thair etlyng euir mar   260
' To ſtand agayne thair fayis mycht,
' Umquhile with ſtrenth, and quhile with flycht,
' And ay thynk to cum to purpos:
' And giff that thaim war ſet in choſs,
' To dey, or to leyff cowartly,   265
' Thai ſuld evar dey chewalruſly.'

Thus gat thaim cunfort the KING;
And, to cunfort thaim, gan in bryng
Auld ſtorys off men that war
Set intill hard aſſayis ſer;   270
And that fortoune cuntraryit faſt,
And come to purpoſs at the laſt.
Tharfor he ſaid, that thai that wald
Thair harts undiſcumfyt hald
Suld ay thynk ententely to bryng   275
All thair enpreſs to gud endyng.
As quhile did CESAR the worthy,
That traweillyt ay ſe beſyly,

With

BUKE III.

With all hys mycht, folowing to mak
To end the purpofs that he wald tak;　280
That hym thocht he had doyne rycht nocht
Ay quhill to do hym levyt ocht:
Forthy gret things efchewyt he,
As men may in hys ftory fe.
Men may fe be hys ythen will,　285
And it fuld als accord to fkill,
That quha taifs purpos fekyrly,
And followis it fyne ententily,
Forowt fayntin, or yheit faynding,
With-thy it be conabill thing,　290
Bot he the mar be unhappy,
He fall efchew it in party.
And haiff he lyff, dayis weill mar fall,
That he fall efchew it all.
For this fuld nane haff difparing　295
For till efchew a full gret thing:
For giff it fall he tharoff failye,
The fawt may be in hys trawailé.

He prechyt thaim on this maner,
And fenyeit to mak better cher,　300
Than he had mattir to be fer:
For hys caufs yeid fra ill to wer.
Thai war ay in fa hard trawaill,
Till the ladyis began to fayle,

Ver. 281, 282. A tranflation of
　Nil actum reputans, fi quid fupereffet agendum.

That mycht the trawaill drey na mar, 305
Sa did othyrs als that thar war.
The Erle IHONE wis ane off tha,
Off ATHOLE, that quhen he faw fua
The KING be difcumfyt twifs,
And fa feile folk agayne him ryfs; 310
And lyff in fic trawaill and dout,
Hys hart begane to faile all out.
And to the KING, apon a day,
He faid, " Gyff I durft to yow fay,
" We lyff into fa mekill dreid, 315
" And haffs oftfyfs off met fik ned,
" And is ay in fic trawailling,
" With cauld, and hungir, and waking,
" That I am fad off myfelwyn fa,
" That I count not my liff a ftra. 320
" Thyr angrys may I ne mar drey,
" For thoucht me tharfor worthit dey,
" I mon foiourne, quharewyr it be,
" Wepys me tharfor per cheryté."
The KING faw that he fa wis failyt, 325
And that he ik wis for trawaillyt.
He faid, " Schyr Erle, we fall fone fe,
" And ordayne how it beft may be.
" Quharewyr ye be, owr Lord yow fend
" Grace, fra your fayis yow to defend." 330
With that in hy to hym callyt he
Thaim, that till hym war maift priué:
Then amang thaim thai thocht it beft
And ordanyt for the liklyeft,

That

That the Queyne, and the erle alſua, 335
And the ladyis, in hy ſuld ga,
With NELE the BRUYSS, to *Kildromy*.
For thaim thocht thai mycht ſekyrly
Duell thar, quhill thai war wictaillit weill:
For ſwa ſtalwart wer the caſtell, 340
That it with ſtrenth war hard to get,
Quhill that tharin wer men and mete.
As thai ordanyt thai did in hy,
The Queyne, and all hyr cumpany,
Lap on thair horſs, and furth thai far. 345
Men mycht haiff ſene, quha had bene thar,
At leve takyng the ladyis gret,
And mak thair face with ters wet:
And knychts, for thair luffs ſak,
Bath ſich, and wep, and murnyng mak: 350
Thai kyſſit thair luffs, at thair partyng.
The KING umbethocht hym off a thing;
That he fra thynce on fute wald ga,
And tak on fute bath weill and wa.
And wald na horſſmen with hym haiff; 355
Tharfor hys borſs all haile he gaiff

Ver. 337. See a curious deſcription of Kildrumy-caſtle, in Mr. Cordiner's valuable *Antiquities and Scenery of the North of Scotland*. The ſtyle of the building is of the twelfth or thirteenth century. It ſtands about thirty miles weſt of Aberdeen, in the country anciently called *Mar*, and was the ſeat of the Earls of Mar. Iſabella, Robert's firſt wife, was daughter of Donald, Earl of Mar; and Chriſtian, ſiſter of Robert, was mother of Regent Mar, ſlain at Dupplin 1332.

To the ladyis, that myſtir had.
The Queyne furth on her way is rade,
And ſawffly come to the caſtell,
Quhar hyr folk war reſawyt weill; 360
And eſyt weill with meyt and drynk.
Bot mycht nane eyſs let hyr to think
On the KING, that wis ſa far ſtad,
That bot Twa Hundir with him had.
The quheyir thaim weill cumfortyt he ay: 365
God help hym, that all mychts may!

The Queyne duelt thus in *Kildromy:*
And the KING, and hys cumpany,
That war twa hundir, and na ma,
Fra thai had ſend thair horſs thaim fra, 370
Wandryt emang the hey muntanys.
Quhar he, and hys, oft tholyt paynys;
For it wis to the wintir ner;
And ſa feile ſayis about him wer,
That all the cuntré thaim werrayit; 375
Sa hard anoy thaim then aſſayit,
Off hungir, cauld, with ſchowrs ſnell,
That nane that levys can weill it tell.

The KING ſaw how hys folk wis ſtad,
And quhat anoyis that thai had, 380
And ſaw wyntir wis cumand ner,
And that he mycht on na wyſs der
In the hillys, the cauld lying,
Na the lang nychts waking.

He

He thocht he to *Kyntyr* wald ga, 385
And fa lang foiowrnyng thar ma,
Till wyntir weddyr war away:
And then he thocht, but mar delay,
Into the manland till arywe,
And till the end hys werds dryw. 390
And for *Kyntyr* lyis in the fe,
Schyr NELE CAMBEL befor fend he,
For to get hym nawyn and meite;
And certane tyme till hym he fete,
Quhen he fuld meite hym at the fe. 395
Schyr NELE CAMBEL, with hys mengye,
Went hys way, but mar letting,
And left hys brothyr with the KING.
And in twalf dayis fua trawaillyt he,
That he gat fchyppyne gud plenté, 400
And wictalis in gret aboundance;
Sa maid he nobill chewifance.
For hys fib men wynnyt tharby,
That helpyt him full wilfully.

The KING, eftir that he wis gane, 405
To *Lowchlomond* the way has tane,
And come thar on the thrid day:
Bot thar about na bait fand thai,
That mycht thaim our the watir ber;
Than war thai wa on gret maner. 410
For it wis fer about to ga;
And thai war into dout alfua,

Ver. 385. Kintyre, the fouthern cherfonefe of Argyle.

To meyt thair fayis that fpred war wyd.
Tharfor, endlang the louch fide,
Sa befyly thai focht, and faft, 415
Tyll IAMYS of DOWGLAS, at the laft,
Fand a litill fonkyn bate,
And to the land it drew ful hate.
Bot it fa litill wis, that it
Mycht our the wattir bot threfum flyt. 420
Thai fend tharoff word to the KING,
That wis joyfull off that fynding;
And fyrft into the bate is gane,
With hym DOWGLAS. The thred wis ane
That rowyt thaim our deliverly, 425
And fet thaim on the land all dry.
And rowyt fa oft fyfs, to and fra,
Fechand ay our twa, and twa,
That in a nycht, and in a day,
Cummyn owt our the louch ar thai. 430
For fum of thaim couth fwome full weill,
And on hys back ber a fardele.
Swa with fwymmyng, and with rowyng,
Thai brocht thaim our, and all thair thing.

The KING, the quhiles, meryly 435
Red to thaim, that war hym by,
Romanys off worthi FERAMBRACE,
That worthily ourcummyn was,

Throw

Ver. 437. I know no Englifh romance of this name; but there is a French one, *Le Roman de Fierabras le Geant*, Geneve, 1478, fol. Cat. Bib. Reg. Gall. Tom. II. N° 142.

This

Throw the rycht douchty OLYWER,
And how the Duk *Peris* wer 440
Affegyt intill *Egrymor*,
Quhar King LAWYNE lay thaim befor,
With ma thoufands then I can fay.
And bot elewyn within war thai,
And a woman: that war fa ftad, 445
That thai na mete tharwithin had,
Bot as thai fra thair fayis wan.
Yheyte fa contenyt thai thaim than,
That thai the tour held manlily,
Tyll that RYCHARD off *Normindy*, 450
Magre his fayis, warnyt the King,
That wis joyfull off this tything:
For he wend thai had all bene flayne.
Tharfor he turnyt in hy agayne,
And wan *Mantrybill*, and paffit *Flagot*, 455
And fyne LAWYNE, and all his flot,

Difpitufly

This romance has been modernized, and is ftill a popular book upon the Pont Neuf at Paris. A copy now lies before me, under the title of *Conqueftes du Grand Charlemagne, Roi de France. Avec les faits heroiques des douze Pairs, et du Grand Fierabras*, &c. *A Troyes, chez Jean Ant. Garnier*; no date, but printed about 1750, 8vo. pp. 175.

The title of Fierabras, like that of many other romances, is improperly given: only fourteen chapters of feventy-feven relating to Fierabras. It is the ftory of the eleven Paladins and Florippa, imprifoned in the tower of Aigremont, by Baland (here called Lawyne) king of the Saracens. The ftory perfectly agrees with Barbour's account; only, ver. 440, for *Duk Peris*, we fhould read, *Duks of Paris*.

Ver. 455. An old Scotifh Tale called *The Brig of the Mantribil,*

Difpitufly difcumfyt he:
And deleuiryt hys men all fre.
And wan the *naylis*, and the *sper*,
And the *crown*, that Ihus couth ber; 460
And off the *croece* a gret party
He wain throw hys chewalry.

The gud KING, upon this maner,
Comfort thaim that war hym ner;
And maid thaim gamyn and folace, 465
Tyll that hys folk all paffyt was.
Quhen thai wer paffit the wattir brad,
Suppofs thai fele of ffayis had,
Thai maid thaim mery, and war blyth;
Not forthy full fele fyth, 470
Thai had full gret defaut off mete,
And tharfor venefoun to get
In twa partyfs ar thai gayne.
The KING hymfelff wis intill ane;
And Schyr JAMES off DOWGLAS 475
Into the tothyr party was.
Then to the hycht thai held thair way,
And huntyt lang quhill off the day;
And focht fchawys, and fets fet;
Bot thai gat litill for till ete. 480

Mantribil, is mentioned in Wedderburn's Complaynt of Scotland, 1549, 12mo.
    Ver. 460. *Ihus* is Jefus.
    Ver. 479. *Schawys*, the thickeft groves in hollows of the wood, where deer are moft apt to be found.—*Sets*, gins or fnares.

BUKE III.

Then hapnyt at that tyme per cafs,
That the Erle of the LENEUAX was
Amang the hillis, ner tharby;
And quhen he hard fa blaw and cry,
He had wondir quhat it my be, 485
And on fic maner fpyrit he,
That knew that it wes the KING:
And then, forowtyn mar duelling,
With all thaim off hys cumpany,
He went rycht till the KING in hy. 490
Sa blyth and fa joyfull, that he
Mycht on na maner blyther be,
For he the KING wend had bene ded,
And he wes alfua will off red,
That he durft not reft into na place. 495
Na fen the KING difcumfyt was
At *Meffan*, he herd newir thing
That euir wis certane off the KING.
Tharfor into full gret daynté,
The KING full humyly haylift he, 500
And he hym welcumyt rycht blythly,
And afkyt hym full tendyrly.
And all the lords, that war thar,
Rycht joyfull off thair meting war,
And kyffyt hym in gret daynté; 505
It wis gret pite for till fe
How thai for joy, and pite gret,
Quhen that thai with thair falows met,

Ver. 507, *Gret* is *weeped*.

That thai wend had bene dede, forthy
Thai welcumyt hym mar hartfully. 510
And he for pité gret agayne,
That neuir off meting was sa fayne.

Thoch I say that thai gret sothly,
It wis na greting propyrly,
For I trow traistly that gretying 515
Cumys to men for mysliking.
And that nane may but angry gret,
Bot it be wemen, that can wet
Thair chekys quheneuir thai list with ters,
The quheyir weill oft thaim nathing ders. 520
Bot I wate weill, but lesyng,
Quhat euir men say of sic greting,
That mekill joy, or yheit peté,
May ger men sua amowyt be,
That wattir fra the hart will ryss, 525
And weyt the eyne on sic a wyss,
That is lik to be greting,
Thoch it be not sua in all thing.
For quhen men grets enkrely,
The hart is sorowfull or angry. 530
Bot for pité I trow gretyng,
Be na thing bot ane opynnyng
Off hart, that schawis the tendirnes
Off rewth that in it closyt is.

The barownys apon this maner, 535
Throw Godd's grace, assemblyt wer,

The

The Erle had mete, and that plenté,
And with glaid hart it thaim gaiff he.
And thai eyt it with full gud will,
That foucht na othyr falſs thartill   540
Bot appetyt, that oft men takys,
For rycht weill fcowryt war thair ſtomakys.
Thai eit, and drank, fic as thai had;
And till our Lord fyne lowyng maid,
And thankyt hym, with full gud cher,   545
That thai war mete on that maner.
The KING than at thaim fperyt yarne,
How thai, fen he thaim feyne, had farne;
And thai full petwyſly gan tell
Auenturs that thaim befell;   550
And gret anoyis, and powerté.
The KING tharat had gret pité.
And tauld thaim petwifly agayne
The noy, the trawaill, and the payne,
That he had tholyt, fen he thaim faw: 555
Wis nane amang thaim, hey na law,
That he ne had pité and plefance,
Quhen that he herd mak remembrance
Off the perellys that paſſyt war.
Bot, quhen men oucht at liking ar,   560
To tell off paynys paſſyt by,
Plefys to herying petiufly,
And to rehearſs thair auld difefe,
Dois thaim oftfyfs cumfort, and efe:

Ver. 561. Et hæc meminiſſe juvabit.

G 3   Withthy

Withthy tharto folow na blame,   565
Difhonour, wikytnes, na fchame.

After the mete fone raifs the KING,
Quhen he had lewyt hys fperyng,
And bufkyt hym, with hys mengye,
And went on hy towart the fe.   570
Quhar Schyr NELE CAMBEL thaim mete,
Bath with fchippis, and with meyte;
Saylys, ayrs, and othyr thing,
That wis fpedfull to thair paffyng.

Then fchippyt thai, forowtyn mar,   575
Sum went till fter, and fum till ar,
And rowyt be the ile of *But*.
Men mycht fe mony frely fute
About the coft, thar lukand,
As thai on ayrs raifs rowand;   580
And nevys that ftallwart war and fquar,
That wont to fpayn gret fpers war,
Swa fpaynyt ars, that men mycht fe
Full oft the hyde leve on the tre.
For all war doand, knycht and knave,   585
Wis nane that euir difport mycht have
Fra fterying, and fra rowyng,
To furthyr thaim off thair fleting.

Bot in the famyn tyme at thai
War in fchippyng, as ye hard me fay,   590
The

BUKE III.

The Erle off the LENEUAX was,
I cannot tell yow throw quhat cafs,
Lewyt behynd with his galay,
Till the KING wis fer on hys way.
Quhen that thai off his cuntré   595
Wyft that fo duelt behynd wis he,
Be fe with fchippys thai hym foucht;
And he that faw that he wis nocht
Off pith to fecht with thefe traytours,
And that he had na ner focours,   600
Then the KINGS flote; forthy
He fped him efter thaim on hy.
Bot the tratours him followit fua,
That thai weill ner hym gan ourta.
For all the mycht that he mycht do,   605
Ay ner, and ner, thai come him to.
And quhen he faw thai war fa ner,
That he mycht weill thair manauce her,
And faw thaim, ner and ner, cum ay,
Then tyll hys mengye gan he fay,   610
' Bot giff we fynd fum futelté,
' Ourtane all fone fall we be.
' Tharfor I rede, but mar letting,
' That, owtakyn owr armyng,
' We caft our all thing in the fe: 615
' And fra our fchip fwa lychtyt be,
' We fall fwa row, and fpeid us fua,
' That we fall weill efchaip thaim fra;
' With that thai fall mak duelling
' Apon the fe, to tak our thing;   620

' And

'And we fall row but refting ay,
'Till we efchapyt be away.'
As he deuifit thai have done;
And thair fchip thai lychtyt fone:
And rowyt fyne, with all thair mycht, 625
And fche, that fwa wis maid tycht,
Rakyt flydand throw the fe.
And quhen thair fayis gan thaim fe,
Forowth thaim alwayis, mar and mar,
The things that thar fletand war 630
Thai tuk; and turnyt fyne agayne,
And be that thai lefyt all thair payne.

Quhen that the Erle on this maner,
And hys mengye, efchapyt wer,
Eftir the KING he gan hym hy, 635
That then, with all hys cumpany,
Into *Kyntyr* arywyt was.
The Erle tauld hym all hys cafs,
How he wis chafyt on the fe,
With thaim that fuld hys awyn be; 640
And how he had bene tane, but dout,
Na war it that he warpyt owt
All that he had, hym lycht to ma:
And fwa efchapyt thaim fra.
"Schyr Erle," faid the KING, "perfay, 645
" Syn yow efchapyt is away,
" Off the tynfell is na plenyeing;
" Bot I will fay the wcile a thing,

" That

" That thar will fall the gret foly
" To paſs oft fra my cumpany.   650
" For feleſyſs, quhen thow art away,
" Thow art ſet in till hard aſſay.
" Tharfor me thynk beſt to thee
" To hald yow alwayis ner by me."
' Schyr,' ſaid the Erle, ' it ſall be ſwa.   655
' I ſall na wiſs paſs fer yow fra,
' Till God giff grace we be off mycht
' Agayne our fayis to hald our flycht.'

And ANGUSS off *Ile* that tyme wis ſyr,
And lord, and ledar of *Kyntyr*.   660
The KING rycht weill reſawyt he ;
And undertuk hys man to be :
And hym, and hys, on mony wiſs,
He abandownyt till hys ſervice.
And, for mar ſekyrnes, gaiff hym ſyne   665
Hys caſtell off *Donabardyne*,
To duell tharin, at hys lyking.
Full gretumly thankyt hym the KING ;
And reſawyt hys ſeruice.
Not forthy, on mony wiſs,   670
He wis dredand for treſoun ay.
And tharefor, as Ik hard men ſay,
He traiſtyt in nane ſekyrly,
Till that he knew hym uterly :

Ver. 659. Angus chief of the ile of Ilay.

Bot

Bot quhat kyndred, that euir he had, 675
Fayr cuntenance to thaim he mad.

And in *Donabardyne* dayis three,
Forowtyne mar, then duellyt he.
Syne gert he hys mengye mak thaim yar,
Towart *Rauchryne*, be se to far. 680
That is ane ile in the se;
And may weill in myd watir be,
Betwix *Kyntyr* and *Irland*:
Quhar als gret ftremys ar rynand,
And als peralais, and mar, 685
Till ourfaile thaim into fchip fair,
As is the raifs of *Bretangye*,
Or ftrait off *Marrock* into *Spanye*.

Thair fchippys to the fe thai fet,
And maid redy, but langir let, 690
Ankyrs, rapys; bath faile, and ar;
And all that nedyt to fchip fair.

Ver. 680. Rachlin, on the north-eaft of Ireland: by Ptolemy called Ricina, by Pliny Ricnia. In the year 635 Segenius Abbot of Hyona, or Icolmkill, founded a church here, which in 795 was burnt by the Danes. *Annal. Tighern. et Ulton.* See a defcription of this iland, and Bruce's caftle, in Hamilton's Obfervations on the North of Ireland.

In the Annals of Ulfter at 768 we find the death of Murgaile Mac Inea, Abbot of Rachlin: at 772 that of Aod Mac Carbre chief of Rachlin.

Quhen

Quhen thai war boune to faile, thai went
The wynd wes weill to thair talent.
Thai rayfyt faile, and furth thai far, 695
And by the mole thai paffyt yar,
And entryt fone into the raffe,
Quhar that the ftremys fa fturdy was,
That wawys wyd, wycht brekand war,
Weltryt as hyllys her and thar. 700
The fchippys our the wawys flayd,
For wynd at poynt blawand thai had;
Bot not forthy quha had thar bene,
A gret ftertling he mycht haiff feyne
Off fchippys; for quhilum fum wald be 705
Rycht on the wawys, as on mounté;
And fum wald flyd fra heycht to law,
Rycht as thai doun till hell wald draw;
Syne on the waw ftert fedanly.
And othyr fchippis, that war tharby, 710
Delivirly drew to the depe.
It wis gret cunningnes to kep
Thair takill intill fic a thrang;
And wyt fic wawis; for ay amang
The wawys reft thair fycht off land. 715
Quhen thai the land wes rycht ner hand,
And quhen fchyppys war failand ner,
The fe wald ryfs on fic maner,
That off the wawys the weltrand hycht
Wald refe thaim oft off thair fycht. 720

Bot

Bot into *Rawchryne*, nocht forthy,
Thai arywyt ilk ane fawffly;
Blyth, and glaid, that thai war fua
Efchapyt the hidwyfs wawys fra.
In *Rauchryne* thai arywyt ar, 725
And to the land thai went but mar,
Armyt apon thair beft maner.
Quhen the folk, that thar wonand wer,
Saw men of armys in thair cuntré,
Aryve into fic quantité, 730
Thai fled on hy, with thar catell,
Towart a rycht ftalwart caftell,
That in the land wis ner tharby.
Men mycht her wemen hely cry,
And fle with cataill her and thar. 735
Bot the KING's folk, that war
Deliuer off fute, thaim gan ourhy;
And thaim areftyt heftely,
And broucht thaim to the KING agayne,
Swa that nane off thaim all wis flayne. 740
Than with thaim tretyt fwa the KING,
That thai, to fullfill hys yarnyng,
Become hys men euirilkane:
And has hym trewly undertane
That thai and thairs, loud and ftill, 745
Suld be in all thing at hys will.
And, quhill him likit thar to leynd,
Euir ilk day thai fuld hym feynd
Wictalis for thre hundir men:
And thai as lord fuld him ken. 750

Bot

Bot at thair poffeffiouns fuld be,
For all hys men thair awyn fre.

   The cunnand on this wyfs wis maid.
And on the morn, but langir baid,
Off all *Rauchrine* bath man and page   755
Knelyt, and maid the KING homage;
And tharwith fwour hym fewté,
To ferve hym ay in lawté.
And held him rycht weill cunnand:
For quhill he duelt into the land,   760
Thai fand meit till hys cumpany;
And ferwyt hym full humely.

THE END OF BUKE III.

THE
BRUCE.

BUKE IV.

ARGUMENT.

The Quene and ladeis are tane prisoneirs be the Inglis.—Kildrumy alsua tane.—King EDWARD I. *advauncing to quell the Scotis, deis at Brugh on Sand.—Ensampil af feynds' prophecies fra Flemish storie.—*DOUGLAS *passes fra Rauchryn to Arran—and after him the* KING, *quha sends a spy to Carrick.—The* KING'S *hostess prophecies his success.—Digressioun on Astrologie and Necromancie.*

THE
BRUCE.

BUKE IV.

IN *Rauchryne* leve we now the KING
In reſt, forowtyn barganyng;
And off hys fayis a quhile ſpek we,
That, throw thair mycht and thair powſté,
Maid ſic a perſecutioune,   5
Sa hard, ſa ſtrait, and ſa feloune,
In thaim that till hym luffand wer
Or kyn, or freynd, or ony maner;
That at till her is gret pité.
For thai ſparyt off na degre   10
Thaim, that thai trowit hys freynd wer,
Nothyr off the kyrk, na ſeculer.
For off *Glaſkow* Byſchop ROBERT,
And MAKIS off *Man* thai ſtythly ſparyt,

Ver. 13. Robert Wiſhart biſhop of Glaſgow from 1272 to 1317, celebrated for his patriotiſm. See Keith's Catalogue of Scotiſh Biſhops. Marcus biſhop of the Iles, 1275 to 1303. *Ibid.* where it is ſaid that he died in 1303, upon no authority; and Barbour here affords proof that he was alive in 1306.

Bath in fetrys and in prefoune; 15
And worthy CRYSTOLL off SEYTOUNE,
Into *Loudon* betrefyt was,
Throw a difcipill off Judas;
MAKNAB, a fals tratour, that ay
Wes off hys duelling, nycht and day; 20
Quhom to he maid gud cumpany.
It wes fer wer than tratoury
For to betryfs fic a perfoune,
So nobill, and off fic renoune.
Bot tharof had he na pité, 25
In hell condampnyt mot he be!
For quhen he hym betryfyt had,
The *Inglifs* men rycht with hym rad
In hy, in *Ingland* to the King,
That gert draw hym, and hede, and hing, 30
Forowtyn peté, or mercy.
It wes gret forow fekyrly,
That fo worthy perfoune as he
Suld on fic maner hangyt be.
Thus gat endyt his worthynes. 35
And off CRAUFURD als Schyr RANALD wes,
And Schyr BRUCE als the BLAIR
Hangyt intill a berne in *Ar*.

 The QUEYNE, and als Dam MAIORY,
Hyr dochtyr, that fyne worthyly 40
Wis coupillyt into Godds band
With WALTIR STEWART off *Scotland*;
        That

Ver. 17. *Lochdoun*: edit.

That wald on na wyſs langar ly
In caſtell off *Kyldromy*,
To byd a ſege, ar rydin raith   45
With knychts and ſquyers bath,
Throw *Roſs*, rycht to the gyrth of *Tayne*.
Bot that trawaill thai maid in wayne.
For thai of *Roſs*, that wald not ber
For thaim na blayme, na yeit danger,   50
Out off the gyrth hame all has tayne,
And ſyne thaim euirilkane
Rycht intill *Ingland*, to the King,
That gert draw all the men, and hing;
And put the Ladyis in preſoune,   55
Sum intill caſtell, ſum in dungeoun.

It wes gret pité for till her
The folk be troublyt on this maner.
That tyme wes in *Kyldromy*,
With men, that mycht war and hardy,   60
Schyr NELE the BRUCE: and I wate weill
That thar the erle wis off ADHEILL,
In the caſtell, weill wictalyt ay,
And mete and fuell gan puruay;
And enforcyt the caſtell ſwa,   65
That thaim thocht na ſtrenth mycht it ta.

Ver. 47. The *gyrth*, or ſanctuary, of St. Duthac at Tain, whence the earl of Roſs took the Queen Elizabeth, daughter of Aymer de Burgh earl of Ulſter, and Marjory the king's daughter by his former wife Iſabella, and delivered them up to the Engliſh.

And quhen it to the King wis tauld
Off *Ingland*, how thai fchup till hauld
That caftell; he wes all angry;
And callyt his fone till hym on hy   70
The eldeft and aperand ayr;
A young bacheler, and ftark, and fayr,
Schyr EDUUARD callyt off *Carnauerane*,
That wes the fterkaft man off ane,
That men mycht in ony cuntré;   75
Prynce of *Walys* that tyme wes he.
And he gert als call erlys twa,
GLOSYSTYR and HARFURD war tha;
And bad thaim wend into *Scotland*,
And fet a fege, with ftalwart hand,   80
To the caftell off *Kyldromy*.
And all the halders halyly
He bad diftroy, forowtyn ranfoun,
Or bryng thaim till hym in prefoune.

Quhen thai the cummaundment had tane,   85
Thai affemblyt ane oft onane,
And to the caftell went in hy;
And it affegyt wigoruſly.
And mony tyme full hard affaylyt;
Bot for to tak it yeit thai failyt.   90
For thai within war rycht worthy;
And thaim defendyt douchtely;
And ruſchyt thair ffayis off agayne,
Sum beft, fum woundyt, fum als flayne.
And mony tymys ifche thai wald,   95
And barganc at the barraifs hald;

And

And wound thair fayis oft and fla.
Schortly thai them contenyt fwa,
That thai withoute difparyt war,
And thoucht till *Ingland* for till far: 100
For thai fa ftyth faw the caftell,
And with that it was warnyft weill;
And faw the men defend thaim fwa,
That thai nane hop had thaim to ta.

Nane had thai done all that fefoune, 105
Gyff it ne had bene fals trefoune.
For thar with thaim wis a tratour,
A fals lourdane, a lofyngeour,
HOSBARNE to name, maid the trefoune,
I wate not for quhat enchefone; 110
Na quham with he maid that conwyn:
Bot as thai faid, that war within,
He tuk a cultir hate glowand,
That yeit wis in a fir brynnand,
And went hym to the mekill hall, 115
That then with corn wis fyllyt all;
And heych up in a mow it did,
Bot it full lang wis nocht thar hid.
For men fayis oft that fyr, na pride,
Bot difcouering may na man hide. 120
For the pomp oft the prid furth fchaws,
Or ellis the gret boift that it blawis.
Na thar may na man fa cowyr
Na low, or rek fall it difcowyr.
So fell it her, for fyr all cler 125
Sone throw the thak burd gan apper,

Fyrſt as a ſterne, ſyne as a mone,
And weill bradder thareſtir ſone,
The fyr out ſyne in bleſs braſt;
And the rek raiſs rycht wondre faſt.   130
The fyr our all the caſtell ſpred,
That mycht na force of man it red.
Than thai within drew to the wall,
That at that tyme was bataillit all,
Within, rycht as it wer withoute.   135
That bataillyne, withowtyn dout,
Sawyt thair lywys, for it brak
Bleſs that thaim wald ourtak.
And quhen the fayis the myſcheiff ſaw,
Till armys went thai in a thraw;   140
And aſſaylyt the caſtell faſt,
Quhar thai durſt come for fyrs blaſt.
Bot thai within myſtir had,
Sa gret defence, and worthy mad,
That thai full oft thair fayis ruflyt,   145
For thai na kyn perall refuſyt.
Thai trawaillyt for to ſauff thair lyffs:
Bot werd, that till the end ay drywis
The warlds things, ſua thaim trawaillyt,
That thai on twa halfys war aſſailyt.   150
In with fyr, that thaim ſwa broilyit;
And utouth with folk, that thaim ſwa toilyit,
That thai brynt magre thaim the yat,
Yat for the fyre, that wis ſwa hate,
Thai durſt not entyr ſwa in hy.   155
Tharfor thar folk thai gan rely,

And

And went to reft, for it wis nycht;
Till on the morn, that day wis lycht,
At fic myfcheiff, as ye her fay,
War thar within the quethyr ay   160
Thai thaim defendyt douchtely,
And contenyt thaim fa manlily,
That or day, throw mekill payn,
Thai had muryt up thair yat agayn.

Bot on the morn, quhen day wes lycht,   165
And fone wes ryffyn, fchynand brycht,
Thai withowt, in hale bataill,
Come purwayt, redy till affaill.
Bot thai within, that fwa war ftad,
That thai wictaill, na fewell had,   170
Quharwith thai mycht the caftell hald,
Tretyt fyrft, and fyne thaim yauld
To be intill the Kings will.
Bot that ay to *Scotts men* wis ill;
As fone eftyr weill wis knawin,   175
For thai war hangyt all and drawyn.

Quhen this cunnand thus tretyt wes,
And affermyt with fekyrnes,
Thai tuk thaim off the caftell fone.
And intill fchort tyme has done,   180
That all a quartir off *Snawdoun*,
Rycht till the erd thai tummyllyt doun.

Syne

Ver. 181. The royal palace at Stirling was called *Snaw-doun*;

Syne towart *Ingland* went thair way.
Bot quhen the King EDUUARD hard fay
How weill the BRUCE held *Kildromy*,　　　185
Agayne hys fon fa ftalwartly;
He gadryt gret chewalry,
And towart *Scotland* went in hy.

And as intill *Northummyrland*
He wis, with hys gret rowt, rydand,　　　190
A feknes tuk hym in the way,
And put hym to fa hard affay,
That he mycht nocht ga, na ryd:
Hym worthit, magre hys, abid
Intill an hamillet tharby,　　　195
A litill town, and unworthy.
With gret payne thyddir thai hym broucht,
He wis fa ftad, that he ne mocht
Hys aynd bot with gret paynys draw;
Na fpek bot giff it war weill law.　　　200
The quheyr he bad thai fuld hym fay
Quhat town wes that, that he in lay.

doun; and near it was an eminence termed Arthur's Round Table. The fame of Arthur in books of chivalry gave rife to fuch names in the middle ages. One of the Heralds of Scotland is termed Snowdun Herald to this day.

Ver. 189. King Edward was obliged by ficknefs to remain in Northumberland and Cumberland, the fummer and autumn 1306; and he was at Lanercoft all the winter 1306-7. See this proved from Rymer's Fœdera in the *Annals of Scotland*, Vol. II. p. 5. He died at Burgh on the Sand, 7 July 1307; and his death is unchronologically here narrated by Barbour.

‘ Schyr,’

' Schyr,' thai faid, ' *Burch in the Sand*
' Men callis this toun, intill this land.'
" Call thai it *Burch*, als ! " faid he ;
" My hop is now fordone to me.
" For I wend neuir to thoile the payne
" Off deid, till I, throw mekill mayn,
" The Burch of Jerufalem had tane,
" My lyff wend I thar fuld be gayne.
" In *Burch* I wyft weill I fuld de :
" Bot I was noythir wys, na fle,
" Till othyr *Burch* kep to ta.
" Now may I nowyfs forthyr ga."

Thus pleynyeit he off hys foly,
As he had mater fekyrly :
Quhen he to wyt certanté
Off that, at nane may certan be.

The quheyr men faid he chefyt had
A fpyryt, that hym anfuer maid,
Off things that he wald inquer.
Bot he fulyt, forowtyn wer,
That gaiff throuch till that creatur.
For feyndys ar off fic natur,
That thai to mankind has inwy ;
For thai wate weill, and wittly,
That thai that weill ar liffand her,
Sall wyn the fege, quharoff thai wer
Tumblyt throwch thair mekill prid.
Quhar throw oft tymys will betid,

That

That quhen feyndys diftrenyeit ar,
For till aper, and mak anfwar,
Throw force off conjuratioun,
That thai fa fals ar and feloun,
That thai mak ay thair anfuering,   235
Into dowbill undirftanding,
To diffaiff thaim, that will thaim trow.
Infample will I fet her now
Off a wer, as I herd tell,
Betwix *Fraunce* and the *Flemyngs* fell.   240

The Erle F*e*RANDS modyr was
Nygramanfour; and Sathanas
Sche rafyt; and hym afkyt fyn,
Quhat fuld worth off the fychtyn
Betwix the *Fraunce* King and hyr fone?   245
And he, as all tyme he wes wone,
Into diffayt maid hys anfuer;
And faid till hyr thir thre werfs her.
" *Rex ruet in bello, tumulique carebit honore,*
" F*e*RRANDUS, Comitiffa, *tuus, mea cara Mi-*
    " *nerva,*   250
" *Parifiis veniet, magna comitante caterva.*"

Ver. 241. Jane, daughter of Baldwin IX. earl of Flanders, married Ferrand prince of Portugal, who thus became earl of Flanders. He took arms againft Philip Auguftus king of France; and the emperor Otho IV. affifting him, in 1214 was fought the famous battle of Bourines, in which the emperor and earl were defeated, and the later carried captive to Paris and confined in the Louvre.

This wis the spek he maid, perfay;
And is in *Inglis* toung to say,
" The King sall fall in the fechting,
" And sall faile honour off erding ;   255
" And thy FERAND, Mynerve my der,
" Sall rycht to *Paryss* went, but wer;
" Folowand hym gret cumpany
" Off nobill men, and off worthy."
This is the sentence off this saw,   260
That the Latyn gan her schaw.
He callyt hyr hys der Minerwe,
For Minerwe ay wis wont serwe
Hym, till sche lessyt at hys diuiss;
And for sche maid the samyn seruice,   265
Hys Minerwe hyr callyt he :
And als, throw hyr sutelté.
He callyt hyr der, hyr tyll dissaiff,
That sche the tyttar suld consaiff
Off hys spek the undyrstanding,   270
That mast plesyt till hyr liking.

This dowbill spek swa hyr dissawyt,
That throw hyr foly the ded ressawit;
For sche wis off hyr ansuer blyth,
And till hyr sone sche tauld it swith.   275
And bad hym till the bataill sped,
For he suld wictory haiff bot dred.
And he, that herd hyr sermonyng,
Sped hym in hy to the fechting;

Quhar

Quhar he diſcomfyt wis, and ſchent;   280
And takin, and to *Paryſs* ſent.
Bot in the fechting not forthy
The King, throw hys chewalry,
Wis laid at the erd, and lawit bath;
Bot his men helpyt hym weill rath.   285

And quhen FERANDS modyr herd
How hyr ſone in the bataill ferd;
And at he ſwa wis diſcomfyt;
Sche raſyt the ill ſpyryt als tyt.
And aſkyt quhy he gabyt had   290
Off the anſuer that he hyr mad?
And he ſaid he had ſaith ſuth all;
" I ſaid the, that the King ſuld fall
" In the bataill; and ſay did he.
" And failyed erding, as men may ſe.   295
" And I ſaid that thy ſon ſuld ga
" To *Paryſs*, and he did richt ſwa;
" Followand ſic a mengye,
" That neuir, in his lyfftyme, he
" Had ſic a mengye in leding.   300
" Now ſeis yow I mad na gabbing."
The wyff confuſyt wis perfay;
And durſt na mar than till hym ſay.

Thus gat, throw dowbill undyrſtanding,
That bargane come till ſic ending,   305
That the ta part diſſawyt was.
Rycht ſa gat fell that in thys caſs:

At

At *Jerusalem* trowyt he
Grawyn in the *Burch* to be;
The quethyr at *Burch into the Sand*   310
He fwelt rycht in hys awn land.

And quhen he to the dede wis ner,
The folk that at *Kyldromy* wer
Come with prifoners that thai had tane,
And fyne to the King are gane.   315
And for to comfort hym thai tauld
How thai the caftell to thaim yauld:
And how thai till hys will war brocht,
To do off that quhateuir he thocht;
And afkyt quhat men fuld off thaim do.   320
Than lukyt he angryly thaim to,
He faid grynnand, "hyngs and drawys."
That wis wondir of fic fawis,
That he, that to the dede wis ner,
Suld anfuer apon fic maner;   325
Forowtyn menyng and mercy.
How mycht he traift on hym to cry,
That futhfaftly demys all thing
To haiff mercy for hys cryng,
Off hym that, throw hys felony,   330
Into fic poynt had na mercy?

Hys men hys maundment has done:
And he deyt thareftir fone:
And fyne wes eftir brocht till berynes.
Hys fone fyne King eftir wes.   335

To the King ROBERT agayne ga we,
That in *Rauchryne*, with hys mengye,
Lay till wintir ner wis gane;
And off that ile hys mete has tane.
JAMYS of DOWGLAS wis angry. 340
That thai langir fuld ydill ly.
And to Schyr ROBERT BOID faid he,
" The pure folk off thys countré
" Ar chargyt apon gret maner,
" Off us, that ydill lyis her. 345
" And Ik her fay, that in *Aràne*,
" Intill a ftyth caftell off ftane,
" Ar *Inglifs* men, that with ftrang hand
" Haldys the Lordfchip off the land.
" Ga we thyddyr; and weill may fall 350
" Amang thaim in fum thing we fall."
Schyr ROBERT faid, ' I grant thartill.
' Till her mar ly war litill fkill:
' Thárfor till *Aran* pafs will we,
' For I knaw rycht weill the cuntré, 355
' And the caftell rycht fwa knaw I.
' We fall come thar fa priwily,
' That thai fall haiff na perfawyng,
' Na yheit wittyng off owr cummyng.
' And we fall ner enbufchyt be, 360
' Quhar we thar outecome may fe.
' Sa fall it on na manir fall,
' Bot fcaith thaim on fum wyfs we fall.

With

With that thai buſkyt thaim anane:
And at the KING thair leiff has tane, 365
And went thaim furth ſyne on thair way.
Into *Kyntyr* ſone cummyn ar thai:
Syne rowyt alwayis by the land,
Till that the nycht wis ner on hand,
Than till *Arane* thai went thar way, 370
And ſawfly thar arywyt thai.
And in a glen thair galay drewch,
And ſyne it halyt weill inewch;
Thair takyll, airs, and thair ſter,
Thai hyde all on the ſamyn maner. 375
And held thair way rycht in the nycht,
Swa that or day wis dawyn lycht,
Thai war enbuſchyt the caſtell ner,
Armyt apon the beſt maner.
And thoucht thai wate war, and wery, 380
And for lang faſtyng all hungry,
Thai thocht till hald thaim all prevé,
Till that thai weill thair poynt mycht ſe.

Schyr IHON the HASTINGS, at that tid,
With knychts off full mekill prid, 385
And ſquyers, and yemanry,
And that a weill gret cumpany,
Was in the caſtell of *Brathwik*.
And oftſyſs quhen it wald hym lik,
He went till huntyng with his menye. 390
And ſwa the land abandownyt he,

That

That durſt nane warne to do hys will.
He was into the caſtell ſtill,
The tyme that JAMES off DOWGLAS,
As Ik haiff tauld, enbuſchit was. 395

Sa hapnyt that tyme, throw chance,
That with wictalis and purweyance,
And with clething, and with armyng,
The day befor, in the ewynnyng,
The under wardane ariuyt was, 400
With thre bats, weill ner the place
Quhar that the folk I ſpak off ar
Preuily enbuſchyt war.
Syne fra the bats ſaw thai ga
Off *Inglis men* threty and ma, 405
Chargit all with ſyndry things;
Sum bar wyne, and ſum armyngs,
The remanent all chargyt wer
With things off ſyndry maner.
And othyr ſyndry yeid thaim by, 410
As thai war maiſtyrs, ydilly.
Thai that enbuſchyt war, that ſaw
All forowtyn dreid or aw,
Thair enbuſchy on thaim thai brak;
And ſlew all that thai mycht ourtak. 415
The cry raiſs hidwyſly, and hey:
For thai, that dredand war to dey,
Rycht as beſts gan rar and cry.
Thai ſlew thaim forowtyn mercy;

Swa

Swa that, into the famyn fted, 420
Weill ner forty ther war dede.

Quhen thai, that in the caftell war,
Hard the folk fa cry and rar,
Thai ifcheyt furth to the fechting.
Bot quhen the DOWGLAS faw thair cummyng, 425
Hys men till hym he gan rely;
And went till meit thaim haftyly.
And quhen thai off the caftell faw
Hym cum on thaim, forowtyn aw,
Thai fled, forowtyn mar debate. 430
And thai thaim folowyt to the yate;
And flew off thaim, as thai in paft;
Bot thai thair yate barryt faft,
That thai mycht do at thaim na mar;
Tharfor thai left thaim ilkane thar, 435
And turnyt to the fe agayne,
Quhar that the men war forowth flayn;
And quhen thai, that war in the bats,
Saw thair cummyng; and faw how gats,
Thai had difcumfyt thair menye, 440
In hy thai put thaim to the fe,
And rowyt faft with all thair mayne:
Bot the wynd wis thaim agayne,
That fwa hey gert the land-bryfs ryfs,
That thai moucht weld the fe nawyfs. 445
Than thai durft not cum to the land,
Bot hald thaim thar fa lang hobland,

That off the thre bats drownyt twa.
And quhen DOWGLAS faw it was fwa,
He tuk armyng, and cleything, 450
Wictalis, wyne, and othyr thing,
That thai fand thar: and held thair way
Rycht glaid and joyfull off thair pray.

Quhen thus JAMES off DOWGLAS,
And hys men, throw Godd's grace, 455
War relewyt with armyng,
And with wictall, and clething,
Syne till a ftrenth thai held thair way;
And thaim full manly gouernyt ay.

Till on the tend day, that the KING, 460
With all that war in hys ledyng,
Arywyt into that countré,
With threty fmall galayis and thre.
The KING arywyt in *Arane*;
And fyne to the land is gane, 465
And in a toune tuk hys herbery.
And fperyt fyne fpeceally,
Gyff ony man couth tell tithand
Off ony ftrang men in that land.
" Yhis," faid a woman, " Schyr, perfay, 470
" Off ftrang men I kan yow fay,
" That are cummyn in this countré,
" And fchort quhile fyne, throw thair bounté,
" Thai haiff difcomfyt owr wardane,
" And mony off hys men has flayne. 475
" And

"And till a ſtalwart place herby
"Repars all thair cumpany."
'Dame,' ſaid the KING, 'wald you me wiſs,
'To that place quhar thair repair is,
'I ſall reward ye but leſing: 480
'For thai ar all off my duelling,
'And I rycht blythly wald thaim ſe,
'And ſwa trow I, that thai wald me.'
"Yhis," ſaid ſche, "Schyr, I will blythly
"Ga with yow and your cumpany,   485
"Till that I ſchaw you thair repair."
'That is inewch, my ſyſtir fayr;
'Now ga we forthwart,' ſaid the KING.
Than went thai furth, but mar letting,
Folowand hyr, as ſche thaim led;   490
Till at the laſt ſche ſchaw't a ſted
To the KING, in a wode glen,
And ſaid, "Schyr, her I ſaw the men,
"That yhe ſper eftir, mak logyng:
"Her I trow be thair reparyng."   495

  The KING then blew his horn in by;
And gert the men that war hym by,
Hald thaim ſtill, and all prewé;
And ſyne agayne his horn blew he.
JAMIS off DOWGLAS herd hym blaw,   500
And at the laſt alſone gan knaw.
And ſaid, "Sothly yon is the KING:
"I knaw lang quhill ſyne hys blawing."

The thred tyme tharwithall he blew,
And then Schyr Robert Boid it knew; 505
And said " Yon is the King, but dreid,
" Ga we furth till hym bettir speid."

Than went thai till the King in hy,
And hym inclynyt curtasly;
And blythly welcummyt thaim the King, 510
And wis joyfull off thair meting.
And kissit thaim; and speryt syne
How thai had farne in thair huntyn?
And thai hym tauld all but lesing:
Syne lowyt thai God off thair meting. 515
Syne with the King till hys herbery
Went bath joyfull and joly.

The King apon the tothyr day
Gan till hys priwé menye say,
" Ye knaw all weill, and ye may se, 520
" How we ar owt off owr cuntré
" Banyst, throw *Inglifs menys* mycht.
" And that, that suld be ours off rycht,
" Throw thair mastyrs thai occupy;
" And wald alsua, forowtyne mercy, 525
" Giff thai haid mycht, destroy us all.
" Bot God forbid it suld sa fall
" Till us, as thai mak manassyng!
" For than war thar na recowering.
" And mankind bidds us that we 530
" To procur wengeance besy be.

" For

" For ye may fe we haiff THRE things
" That maks us oft moneſtings
" For to be worthy, wyſs, and wycht,
" And till anoy thaim at our mycht.   535
" ANE is our lyffs fawfté,
" That on na wyſs fuld fawft be,
" Giff thai had us at thair liking.
" The TOTHYR that makys eggyng,
" Is that thai our poſſeſſioune   540
" Halds ſtrenthly, agayn refoune.
" The THRID is the joy that we abid,
" Gyff that it happyn, as weill may tid,
" That we wyn wictour, and maiſtry
" Till ourcum thair felony.   545
" Tharfor we fuld our harts raiſs,
" Swa that na myſcheyff us abaiſs;
" And ſchaip alwayis to that ending
" That bers in it menſk, and lowing.
" And tharfor, lordings, gyff ye fe   550
" Amang you, giff that it ſpeidfull be,
" I will fend a man in *Carrik*,
" To fpy and fpeir our kynrik,
" How it is led, and freynd and fa.
" And giff he feis we land may ta,   555
" On *Turnberys Inuke* he may
" Mak a fyr, on a certane day,
" That mak takynnyng till us, that we
" May thar arywe in fawfté.
" And giff he feis we may not fwa;   560
" Luk on na wyſs the fyr he ma.

I 3   " Swa

" Swa may we tharthrow haiff wittring
" Off our paſſage, or our duelling."

To this ſpek all aſſentyt ar.
And than the KING, withowtyn mar,   565
Callyt ane, that wes hym prewé,
And off *Carrik* hys countré.
And chargyt hym in les and mar,
As ye hard me diwiſs it ar.
And ſet hym certain day to ma   570
The fyr, giff he ſaw it war ſwa
That thai had poſſibilité
To maynteyne the wer in that countré.

And he, that wis rycht weill in will
His lord's yharnyng to fullfill,   575
As he that worthy wis, and leile,
And couth rycht weill ſecrets conſeill;
Sake wis boune intill all thing
For to fullfill hys cummanding.
And ſaid he ſuld do ſa wiſely,   580
That na repruff ſuld eftir ly.
Syne at the KING hys leiff has tane;
And furth apon hys way is gane.

Now gais the meſſynger hys way,
That hat CUTBERT, as I herd ſay.   585
In *Carrik* ſone arywyt he,
And paſſyt throw all the countré.

Bot

Bot he fand few tharin, perſay,
That gud wald off hys maiſtir ſay:
For fele of thaim durſt not for dreid; 590
And othyr ſum rycht into deid
War ſayis to the nobill KING,
That rewyt ſyne thair bargaynyng.
Baith hey and law, the land wis then
All occupyt with *Ingliſſmen*; 595
And diſpytyt, at-our all thing,
ROBERT the BRUCE the douchty KING.
Carrik wis giffyn then halyly
To Schyr HENRY Lord the PERSY;
That in *Turnberyis* caſtell then 600
Was, with weill ner three hundir men.
And dawntyt ſa gat all the land,
That all wis till hym obeyſand.

Thus CUTBERT ſaw thair felony:
And ſaw the folk ſa halyly 605
Be worthyn *Ingliſs*, baith rich and pur,
That he to nane durſt hym diſcur.
Bot thoucht to leve the fyr unmaid:
Syne till hys maiſter went but baid,
And all thair cowyne till hym gan tell, 610
That wis ſa angry and ſa fell.

The

Ver. 606. By *being become Engliſh* our poet only implies that they were attached to the Engliſh cauſe.

Ver. 609, 610. The expreſſions are inaccurate, but do
not

The KING, that intill *Arane* lay,
Quhen that cummyn wis the day,
That he fet till hys meffenger,
As Ik dewifyt you lang er, 615
Eftyr the fyr he lukyt faft.
And, als fone as the none was paft,
Hym thocht weill he faw a fyr,
Be *Turnbery* byrnand weill fchyr;
And till hys menye it gan fchaw: 620
Ilk man thocht weill that he it faw.
Then with blyth hart the folk gan cry,
‘ Gud KING! fpeid you deliuerly,
‘ Swa that we fone in the ewynnyng
‘ Aryve, forowtyn perfaywing.’ 625
“ I grant,” faid he, “ now mak you yar.
“ God furthyr us intill our far!”

Then in fchort tyme men mycht thaim fe
Schute all thair galayis to the fe,
And ber to fe baith ayr and fter, 630
And othyr things that myftir wer.
And as the KING apon the fand
Was gangand up and down, bidand
Till that hys menye redye war,
Hys oft come rycht till hym thar. 635
And quhen that fche hym halyft had,
A priwé fpek till hym fche made;

not mein that Cuthbert went to the king, but only that he intended to go, as appears from the fequel.

And

And faid, "Takis gud kep till my faw,
"For or ye pafs I fall you fchaw,
"Off your fortoun a gret party.   640
"Bot our all fpecially
"A wyttring her I fall yow ma,
"Quhat end that your purpofs fall ta.
"For in this land is nane trewly
"Wate things to cum fa weill as I.   645
"Ye pafs now furth on your wiage,
"To wenge the harme, and the owtrage,
"That *Ingliffmen* has to yow done;
"Bot yow wat not quhat kyne forton
"Ye mon drey in your werraying.   650
"Bot wyt ye weill, withoutyn lefing,
"That fra ye now haiff takyn land,
"Nane fa mychty, na fa ftrenthtlie of hand,
"Sall ger yow pafs owt of your countré
"Till all to yow abandownyt be.   655
"Within fchort tyme ye fall be KING,
"And haiff the land to your liking,
"And ourcum your fayis all.
"Bot fele anoyis thole ye fall,
"Or that your purpofs end haiff tane;   660
"Bot ye fall thaim ourdryve ilkane.
"And, that ye trow this fekyrly,
"My twa fonnys with yow fall I
"Send to tak part of your trawaill;
"For I wate weill thai fall not faill   665
"To be rewardyt weill at rycht,
"Quhen ye ar heyit to your mycht."

         The

The KING, that herd all hyr carping,
Thankyt hyr in mekill thing,
For sche cumfort hym sum deill,   670
The quheyir he trow that not full weill
Hyr spek, for he had gret ferly
How sche suld wyt it sekyrly.
As it was wondirfull perfay
How ony manys science may   675
Knaw things that ar to cum,
Determynabilly, all or sum.
Bot giff that he infpyrit war
Off hym, that all thing euirmar
Seyis in hys prefens.   680
As was DAUID, and JEREMY,
SAMUELL, JOELL, and YSAI,
That at, throw his haly grace, gan tell
Fele things that eftir fell.
Bot the prophets sa thyn ar sawyn,   685
That nane in erd now is knawyn.

Bot fele folk ar sa curyous,
And to wyt things cowatous,

Ver. 668. Robert may perhaps have used a stratagem in this business, to encourage his adherents; for as he had all the prowess of an ancient hero, so he had all the wisdom, and art, and consummate policy. This old woman may have been to him as Egeria to Numa, or the white hind to Sertorius.

Ver. 687. Our poet here goes into a digression, very sensible for the time, on astrology, and thence passes to necromancy, ver. 747.

That

That thai, throw thair gret clergy,
Or ellys throw thair dewilry, 690
On thir twa maners maks fanding
Off things to cum to haiff knawing.
Ane off thaim is aftrologi,
Quhar clerkys, that ar witty,
May knaw conjounctions off planets, 695
And quheyir that thair courfs thaim fetts,
In foft fegs, or in angry;
And off the hewyn all halyly
How that the difpofitioun
Suld apon things wyrk hyr doun; 700
On regiones, or on climats,
That wyrkys not ay quhar agats,
Bot fum quhar lefs, and fum quhar mar,
Eftyr as thair bemys ftrekyt ar,
Othir all ewyn, or on wry. 705
Bot me thinks it war gud maiftry
Till ony aftrolog to fay
This fall fall her, and on this day.
For thoucht a man hys lyff haly
Studyt fwa in aftrology, 710
That on fternys hys hewid he brak,
The wyfs man fayis he fuld not mak
All hys lyff certane, dayis thre;
And yheit fuld he ay doute quhill he
Saw how that it come till endyng; 715
Than is that na certane demyng.
Or giff the men, that will ftudy
In the craft off aftrology,

Knaw

Knaw all menys natioun,
And knew the conſtellatioun   720
That kynd lik maners gifs thai till,
For to inclyne to gud or ill;
How that thai throw ſcience of clergi,
Or throw ſlycht off aſtrology,
Couth tell quhat kyn perill appers,   725
To thaim that haldys kynd lik maners;
I trow that thai ſuld faile to ſay
The things that thaim happyn may.
For quhethir ſa men inclynit be
To vertue, or to mawyté,   730
He mycht rycht weill refrenye hys will,
Othir throw nurtur, or throw ſkill:
And to the contrar turne hym all.
And men has mony tyme ſene fall
That men kyndly till ill will gewyn,   735
Throw thair gret wit away has drewyn
Thair ill; and worthin off gret renoun
Magre the conſtellatioun.
As Aristotill, giff as men redys,
He had folowyt hys kyndly deds,   740
He had bene fals and cowatouſs;
Bot hys wyt maid hym vertuouſs.
And ſen men may on this kyn wyſs
Wyrk agayne that courſs, that is
Pryncipaill cauſs off thair demyng,   745
Methink thair deyme na certane thing.

Nygromancy

Nygromancy the othyr is,
That kennys men on fyndry wyfs,
Throw ftalwart conjourationys,
And throw exortiyationys, 750
To ger fpyrits to thaim apper,
And giff anfuers on fer maner.
As quhylum did the Phitones,
That quhen SAUL abayfyt wes
Off the *Phelyftynys'* mycht, 755
Rayfyt, throw hyr mekill flycht,
SAMUEL's fpyrite als tite,
Or in hys fted the iwill fpyrite,
That gaiff rycht graith anfuer hyr to.
Bot off hyrfelff rycht nocht wyft fche. 760
And man is into dreding ay
Off things that he has herd fay;
Namly off things to cum quhill he
Knaw off the end the certanté.
And fen thai ar in fic wenyng, 765
Forowtyne certanté off wytting,
Methink quha fayis he knawis things
To cum, he makys gret gabbings.

Bot quheythir fche that tauld the KING
How hys purpofs fuld tak ending, 770
Wenyt, or wyft it uttirly,
It fell eftir all halyly
As fche faid. For fyne KING was he;
And off full mekill renounné.

THE END OF BUKE IV.

THE

THE
BRUCE.

BUKE V.

ARGUMENT.

The KING *arrives in Carric; and with four hundred men beginnis the deliveraunce of his kingrik fra the Inglis garrisouns.—Schir* HENRY *de* PERSY *flees.—*DOUGLAS *be stratagem taks his awin castel in Douglasdale.—Schir* AYMER *de* VALLANGE *sends* UMFRAVILLE *till quell the* KING. — UMFRAVILLE *bribis three of the* KING'S *men to murder him, bot he kills the traitours.*

THE
BRUCE.

BUKE V.

THIS wis in ver, quhen winter tid,
With hys blafts hydwyfs to bide,
Was ourdrywyn: and birds fmale,
As turtule and the nychtyngale,
Begouth rycht fariolly to fyng; 5
And for to mak in thair fingyng
Swete nots, and fownys fer,
And melodys plefand to her.
And trees begouth to ma
Burgeans, and brych blomys alfua, 10
To wyn the helying off thair hewid,
That wykkyt wyntir had thaim rewid.
And all greffys begouth to fpryng.
Into that tyme the nobill KING,
With hys flote, and a few mengye, 15
THRE HUNDIR I trow thai mycht be,

Ver. 1. Spring, 1307. *Ver* is Icelandic as well as Latin for fpring. The defcription is pretty.

Is to the se, oute off *Arane*,
A litill forouth ewyn gane.

 Thai rowyt fast, with all thair mycht,
Till that apon thaim fell the nycht,   20
That woux myrk apon gret maner,
Swa that thai wyst not quhar thai wer.
For thai na nedill had, na stane;
Bot rowyt alwayis intill ane,
Styrand all tyme apon the fyr,   25
That thai saw brynand lycht and schyr.

 It was bot auentur thaim led:
And thai in schort tyme sa thaim sped,
That at the fyr arywyt thai;
And went to land bot mar delay.   30
And CUTBERT, that has sene the fyr,
Wis full off angyr, and off ire;
For he durst not do it away;
And wis alsua dowtand ay
Thai hys lord suld pass to se,   35
Tharfor thair cummyn waytit he:
And met thaim at thair arywing.
He wis weile sone broucht to the KING,
That speryt at hym how he had done.
And he with sar hart tauld hym sone,   40
How that he fand nane weill lyffand,
Bot all war fayis, that he fand.
And that the Lord the PERSY,
With ner thre hundir in cumpany,

         Was

Was in the caſtell thar beſid, 45
Fullfellyt off diſpyt and prid.
Bot ma than twa parts off hys rowt
War herberyt in the toune without;
" And diſpytyt yow mar, Schir KING,
" Than men may diſpyt ony thing." 50
Than ſaid the KING, in full gret ire,
' Tratour, quhy maid yow than the fyr?'
" A! Schyr," ſaid he, " ſa God me ſe!
" The fyr wis newyr maid for me.
" Na, or the nycht, I wyſt it not; 55
" Bot fra I wyſt it weill I thocht
" That ye, and haly your mengye,
" In hy ſuld put yow to the ſe.
" Forthy I cum to mete yow her,
" To tell perills that may apper." 60

The KING wes off hys ſpek angry,
And aſkyt hys priwé men, in hy,
Quhat at thaim thocht wes beſt to do.
Schyr EDUUARD fryſt anſueryt tharto,
Hys brodyr that wis ſwa hardy, 65
And ſaid; " I ſay yow ſekyrly

" Thar

Ver. 45. The caſtle of Turnberry in Carrick, the patrimonial country of Bruce, whoſe anceſtors were earls of Carrick; and who thence expected to find the people there more attached to him, than thoſe of any other part of Scotland.

Ver. 65. Prince Edward's character will appear to the reader, from the account of his actions in Ireland detailed in this

" Thar fall na perill, that may be,
" Dryve me eftfonys to the fe.
" Myne auentur her tak will I,
" Quhethir it be esfull or angry."   70
' Brodyr,' he faid, ' fen yow will fua,
' It is gud that we famyn ta,
' Diffefe or efe, or payne or play,
' Eftyr as God will us purway.
' And fen men fay that the PERSY   75
' Myne heritage will occupy;
' And hys menye fa ner us lyis,
' That us difpyts mony wyfs;
' Ga we, and wenge fum off the difpyt.
' And that may we haiff done als tite;   80
' For thai ly traiftly, but dreding
' Off us, or off owr her cummyng.
' And thouch we fleping flew thaim all,
' Repruff tharof na man fall.
' For werrayour na forfs fuld ma,   85
' Quheythir he mycht ourcum his fa
' Throw ftrenth, or throw futelté;
' Bot that gud faith ay haldyn be.'

Quhen this wis faid thai went thair way;
And to the toune fone cummyn ar thai,   90
Sa priwily, but noyifs making,
That nane perfawyt thair cummyng.

this poem, to have been bold to excefs, and untempered by the prudence which fhines in that of his brother the king.
Ver. 87. *Dolus an virtus, quis in hofte requirit.*

Thai

Thai íkalyt throw the towne in hy;
And brak up durs íturdely,
And ílew all that thai mycht ourtak; 95
And thai, that na defence moucht mak,
Full petowíly gan rar and cry;
And thai ílew thaim diípitowíly.
As thai that war in full gud will
To wenge the angyr, and the ill, 100
That thai, and thairs, had thaim wrocht;
With ía feloun will thaim íoucht,
That thai ílew thaim euir ilkane,
Owtane MAKDOWELL hym allane,
That eíchapyt, throw gret ílycht, 105
And throw the myrknes off the nycht.

In the caítell the Lord the PERSY
Hard weill the noyis, and the cry:
Sa did the men, that within wer,
And full effraytly gat thair ger. 110
Bot off thaim wis nane ía hardy,
That euir iíchyt fourth to the cry.
In íic effray thai baid that nycht,
Till on the morn, that day wes lycht;
And than íeíyt into party 115
The noyis, the ílawchtyr, and the cry.

The KING gert be depertyt then
All hale the reff amang the men,
And duellyt all ítill thar dayis thre.
Sic hanfell to that folk gaiff he, 120

Rycht in the fyrſt beginnyng,
Newlings at hys arywyng.

 Quhen that the KING, and hys folk, war
Arywyt, as I tauld yow ar,
A quhill in *Karryk* leyndyt he,   125
To ſe quha freynde, or fa, wald be,
Bot he fand litill tendyrneſs.
And nocht forthy the puple wes
Inclynyt till hym in party;
Bot *Ingliſs men* ſa angrely   130
Led thaim with daunger, and with aw,
That thai na freyndſchip durſt hym ſchaw.
Bot a lady off that cuntré,
That wis till hym in ner degre
Off coſynage, wis wondir blyth   135
Off hys arywyng; alſwyth
Sped hyr till hym, in full gret hy,
With fourty men in cumpany:
And betaucht thaim all to the KING,
Till help hym in hys werraying.   140
And he reſawyt thaim in daynté,
And hyr full gretly thankyt he;
And ſperyt tythands off the QUEYNE,
And off hys freynds all bedene,
That he had left in that countré,   145
Quhen that he put hym to the ſe.
And ſche hym tauld, ſichand full ſar,
How that hys brothyr takyn war

             In

In the caſtell off *Kyldromy*,
And deſtroyit ſa welanyſly: 150
And the Erle of ATHALL alſua.
And how the QUEYNE, and othyr ma,
That till hys party wer heldand,
War tane, and led in *Ingland*,
And put in feloun priſoune.   155
And how that CRISTOLE off SETOUN
Was ſlayn, gretand ſche tauld the KING,
That ſorowfull wes off that tithing.
And ſaid, quhen he had thocht a thraw,
Thir words, that I ſall yow ſchaw.   160
" Allace," he ſaid, " for luff off me,
" And for thair mekill lawté,
" Thaiſe nobill men, and thaiſe worthy,
" Ar deſtroyit ſa welanyſly!
" Bot and I leyff in lege powyſté,   165
" Thar deid rycht weill ſall wengyt be.
" The King the quheyr off *Ingland*
" Thocht that the kynryk off *Scotland*
" Was to litill to thaim, and me,
" Tharfor he will it myn all be.   170
" Bot off gud CRISTOLE off SETOUN,
" That was off ſa nobill renoun,
" That he ſuld dey war gret pité,
" Bot quhar worſchip myt prowyt be.

 Ver. 151. The earl of Athole was executed as a traitor at London. See *Annals*, ii. 14.
 Ver. 156. Sir Chriſtopher Seton, who had married the king's ſiſter, was executed at Dumfries. *Ibid.*

The King fichand thus maid hys mayn; 175
And the lady hyr leyff has tayne:
And went hyr hame till hyr wennyng.
And fele fyfs comfort the KING
Bath with filuer, and with mete,
Sic as fche in the land mycht get. 180

And he oft ryot all the land,
And maid all hys that euir he fand;
And fyne drew hym till the hycht,
To ftynt bettir hys fayis mycht.

In all that tyme wis the PERSY, 185
With a full fympill cumpany,
In *Turnberyfs* caftell lyand,
For the King ROBERT fwa dredand,
That he durft not ifch furth to fayr
Fra thence to the caftell off *Ayr*, 190
That wis then full off *Inglifmen*;
Bot lay lurkand as in a den.
Till the men off *Northummyrland*
Suld cum armyt, and with ftrang hand
Conwoy hym till hys cuntré, 195
For hys faynd till thaim fend he.
And thai in hy affemblyt then,
Paffand, I weyne, a thoufand men;
And afkyt awifement thaim amang,
Quheythir that thai fuld duell or gang, 200

Bot

Bot thai war skowurand wondir sar,
Sa far into *Scotland* for to far.
For a knycht, Schyr GAWTER the LELE,
Said it wis all to gret perill
Sa ner thir sodjourys to ga. 205
This spek discomfort thaim swa,
That thai had left all thair wyage,
Na war a knycht off gret corage,
That Schyr ROGER off SAINT IHON hycht,
That thaim comfort with all hys mycht. 210
And sik words to thaim gan say,
That thai all samyn held thair way
Till *Turnbery*, quhar the PERSY
Lap on, and went with thaim in hy
In *Ingland* hys castell till, 215
Forowtyne distrowblyne or ill.

Now in *Ingland* is the PERSY,
Quhar I trow he a quhill sall ly,
Or that he schap hym for to fayr
To werray *Carryk* ony mar. 220
For he wyst he had na rycht;
And als he dreid the KINGS mycht,
That in *Carryk* wes trawailland,
In the maist strenth off the land.

Quhar JAMYS off DOWGLAS, on a day, 225
Come to the KYNG, and gan hym say,
" Schyr, with your leve, I wald ga se
" How that thai do in my cuntré;

" And

"And quhow my men demanyt ar.
"For it annoyis me wondir far   230
"That the CLYFFURD, fa pefabylly,
"Brukys and haldys the fenyowry,
"That fuld be myne with all kyn rycht.
"Bot quhill I lyff, and may haiff mycht
"To lede a yowman, or a fwayne,   235
"He fall not bruk it but bargayne."
The KING said, 'Certs I cannot fe
'How that yow yhet may fekyr be
'Into that countré for to far,
'Quhar *Inglifs men* fa mychty ar;   240
'And yow wate nocht quha is thy freynd.'
He faid, "Schyr, nedways I will wend,
"And tak the auentur God will gyff,
"Quithyr it be to dey or lyff."
The KING said, 'Sen it is fwa,   245
'That you fic yarnyng has to ga,
'Yow fall pafs furth with my blyffing.
'And giff the hapnys ony thing
'That anoyis or fcaithfull be,
'I pray ye fped ye fone to me;   250
'And tak we famyn quhateuir may fall.'
"I grante," he faid: and tharwithall
He lowtyt; and hys leve has tane.
And towart hys cuntré is he gane.

Now takys JAMES hys wiage   255
Towart *Dowglas*, hys heritage,

With

With twa yemen, forowtyn ma;
That wis a simple stuff to ta,
A land or a castell to wyn.
The quhcyr he yarnyt to begyn 260
To bring purpoſs till ending;
For gud help is in gud begynnyng.
For gud begynnyng, and hardy,
Giff it be folowit wittily,
May ger oftſyſs unlikly thing 265
Cum to full conabill ending.
Swa did it her; bot he wis wyſs,
And ſaw he mycht, on na kyn wyſs,
Werray hys ſa with ewyn mycht,
Tharfor he thocht to wyrk with ſlycht. 270
And in *Dowglaſdale*, hys cuntré,
Apon an cwynnyng entryt he.
And then a man wonnyt tharby,
That was off freynds weill mychty,
And rych of moble, and off cateill; 275
And had bene till hys fadyr leill;
And till hymſelff, in hys youthed,
He haid done mony a thankfull deid.
THOM DICSON wis hys name perfay.
Till hym he ſend; and gan hym pray 280
That he wald cum all allenarly,
For to ſpek with hym priuely.
And he bot daunger till hym gais;
Bot fra he tauld hym quhat he wais,
He gret for joy, and for pité, 285
And hym rycht till hys houſs had he.

Quhar

Quhar in a chambre priuely
He held hym, and hys cumpany,
That nane had off hym perſawing.
Off mete, and drink, and othyr thing,   290
That mycht thaim eyſs, thai had plenté.
Sa wroucht he throw ſutelté,
That all the lele men off that land,
That with hys fadyr war duelland,
This gud man gert cum, ane and ane,   295
And mak hym manrent euir ilkane,
And he hymſelff fyrſt homage maid.
DOWGLAS in hart gret glaidſchip haid,
That the gud men off hys cuntré
Wald ſwagate till hym bounden be.   300
He ſperyt the conwyne off the land,
And quha the caſtell had in hand.
And thai hym tauld all halyly;
And ſyne amang thaim priuily
Thai ordanyt, that he ſtill ſuld be   305
In hiddillis, and in priweté,
Till Palme Sonday, that wis ner hand,
The thrid day eftyr folowand.
For than the folk off that cuntré
Aſſemblyt at the kyrk wald be,   310
And thai, that in the caſtell wer,
Wald als be thar thair palmys to ber;
As folk that had na dred of ill;
For thai thocht all wis at thair will.
Than ſuld he cum with hys twa men,   315
Bot, for that men ſuld not hym ken,

He

He fuld a mantill haiff auld and bar,
And a flaill, as he a threfscher war.
Undir the mantill not forthy
He fuld be armyt priuely.   320
And quhen the men off hys cuntré,
That fuld all boune befor hym be,
Hys enfonye mycht her hym cry,
Then fuld thai full enforcely,
Rycht in the myddys the kirk, affaill   325
The *Inglifmen* with hard bataill,
Swa that nane mycht efchaip tharfra;
For tharthrouch trowyt thai to ta
The caftell, that befid wis ner.
And quhen thys, that I tell yow her,   330
Was deuifyt, and undirtane,
Ilk ane till hys houfs hame is gane;
And held this fpek in priuity,
Till the day off thair affembly.

The folk apon the fermoun day   335
Held to Sayint Brids kyrk thair way;

Ver. 317. The clofe veft with fleeves, and mantle or cloke over it, in the Spanifh fafhion, were long the drefs of the men in Scotland, poor as well as rich. See *Peblis to the Play*, and other old Scotifh poems.

Ver. 323. The *enfigny* was the word of war, generally the name of the leader.

Ver. 336. The Irifh Saint Brigit was much revered in Scotland: and one of the earlieft churches in the country was dedicated to her. See the *Chronicon Piɛtorum* in Innes's Effay.

Palm-funday was the 19th of March, in 1307.

And

And thai that in the caftell war
Ifchyt owt, bath les and mar,
And went thair palmys for to ber;
Owtane a cuk and a porter. 340

JAMES off DOWGLAS off thair cummyng,
And quhat thai war, had witting.
And fped hym till the kyrk in hy;
Bot or he come, to haftily
Ane off hys cryt, DOWGLAS! DOWGLAS! 345
THOMAS DICKSON, that nerreft was
Till thaim that war off the caftell,
That war all innouth the chancell,
Quhen he DOWGLAS! fwa hey herd cry,
Drew owt hys fwerd; and fellely 350
Rufchyt amang thaim to and fra;
Bot ane or twa, forowtyn ma,
Then in hy war left lyand,
Quhill DOWGLAS come rycht at hand.
And then enforcyt on thaim the cry; 355
Bot thai the chanfell fturdely
Held, and thaim defendyt wele,
Till off thair men wis flayne fum dell.
Bot the DOWGLAS fwa weill hym bar,
That all the men, that with hym war, 360
Had comfort off hys weill doying;
And he hym fparyt na kyn thing,
Bot prowyt fa hys force in fycht,
That throw hys worfchip, and hys mycht,

Hys

Hys men fa keynly helpyt than, 365
That thai the chanfell on thaim wan.
Than dang thai on fa hardely,
That in fchort tyme men mycht fe ly
The twa part dede, or than deand.
The lave war fefyt fone in hand. 370
Swa that off threty levyt nane,
That thai ne war flayne ilkan, or tane.

JAMES off DOWGLAS, quhen this wis done,
The prifoners has he tane alfone;
And, with thaim off hys cumpany, 375
Towart the caftell went in hy,
Or noyifs, or cry, fuld ryfs.
And for he wald thaim fone furpryfs,
That lewyt in the caftell war,
Thai war but twa forowtyn mar, 380
Fyve men, or fex, befor fend he,
That fand all opyn the entré.
And entryt, and the porter tuk
Rycht at the yate, and fyne the cuk.
With that DOWGLAS come to the yate, 385
And entryt in, forowtyn debate;
And fand the mete all redy grathit,
With burdys fet, and clathis layit.
The yhatts then he gert fper,
And fat, and eyt all at layfer. 390
Syne all the guds turffyt thai,
That thaim thocht thai mycht haiff away.

And

And manly wapnys, and armyng,
Siluer, and tresour, and clethyng;
Wyctallis, that mycht nocht turſyt be, 395
On this maner deſtroyit he;
All the wictallis owten ſalt,
Als quheyt, and flour, and meill, and malt,
In the wyne ſellar gert he bring;
And ſamyn on the flur all flyng. 400
And the priſoners that he had tane
Rycht tharin gert he heid ilkane;
Syne off he townnys the heids outſtrak;
A foule mellé thar gane he mak.
For meill, and malt, and blud, and wyne, 405
Ran all togeddyr in a mellyne,
That wes unſemly for to ſe.
Tharfor the men off that countré
For ſwa fele thar mellyt wer,
Callyt it the *Dowglas Lardner*. 410
Syne tuk he ſalt, as I hard tell,
And ded horſs, and ſorded the well.
And brynt all, outakyn ſtane;
And is forth, with hys mengye, gayne
Till hys reſett; for hym thocht weill, 415
Giff he had haldyn the caſtell,
It had bene aſſegyt raith;
And that hym thocht to mekill waith.
For he ne had hop off reſkewyng.
And it is to peralous thing 420

Ver. 403. He daſhed off the tops of the tuns of wine.

In

In caſtell aſſegyt to be,
Quhar want is off thir things thre,
Wictaill, or men with thair armyng,
Or than gud hop off reſcuyng.
And for he dred thir things ſuld faile, 425
He cheſyt furthwart to trawaill,
Quhar he mycht at hys larges be;
And ſwa dryve furth hys deſtané.

On this wyſe wis the caſtell tan,
And ſlayne that war tharin ilkane. 430
The DOWGLAS ſyne all hys menye
Gert in ſer placis depertyt be;
For men ſuld wyt quhar thai war,
That yeid depertyt her and thar.
Thaim that war wowndyt gert he ly 435
Intill hiddillis, all priuely;
And gert gud leches till thaim bring,
Quhill that thai war intill heling.
And hymſelff, with a few menye,
Quhile ane, quhile twa, and quhile thre, 440
And umquhill all hym allane,
In hiddilis throw the land is gane.
Sa dred he *Ingliſs mennhys* mycht,
That he durſt not weile cum in ſycht.
For thai war that tyme all weldand 445
As maiſt lords, our all the land.

Bot tythands, that ſcals ſone,
Off this deid that DOWGLAS has done,

Come

Come to the CLIFFURD his ere, in hy,
That for his tynſaill was ſary;   450
And menyt hys men that thai had ſlayne.
And ſyne has to purpoſs tane,
To big the caſtell up agayne.
Tharfor, as man of mekill mayne,
He aſſemblyt gret cumpany,   455
And till *Dowglas* he went in hy.
And biggyt up the caſtell ſwyth;
And maid it rycht ſtalwart and ſtyth;
And put tharin wictallis, and men.
Ane off the THYRWALLYS then   460
He left behind hym capitane,
And ſyne till *Ingland* went agayne.

Into *Carryk* yis the KING,
With a full ſymple gadryng;
He paſſyt not TWA HUNDER men.   465
Bot Schyr EDUUARD, hys brodyr, then
Wes in *Galloway*, weill ner hym by,
With hym ane othyr cumpany,
That held the ſtrenthis off the land.
For thai durſt not yeit tak on hand   470
Till ourrid the land planly.
For off WALENCE Schyr AMERY
Was intill *Edynburgh* lyand,
That yeit was wardane off the land,

Ver. 463. The eaſtern woods and wilds of Carrick were long the refuge of our hero.

Undirneyth

Unditneyth the *Inglifs* King. 475
And quhen he herd off the cummyng
Off King ROBERT, and hys mengye,
Into *Carryk*; and how that he
Haid flayne off the PERSYS men;
Hys cunfaill he affemblyt then. 480
And, with affent off hys cunfaill,
He fent till *Ar*, hym till affaill,
Schyr INGRAME BELL, that wis hardy,
And with him a gret cumpany.

And quhen Schyr INGRAME cummyn wis thar,
Hym thocht not fpeidfull for till far, 486
Till affaile hym into the hycht.
Tharfor he thocht to wyrk with flycht;
And lay ftill in the caftaill than,
Till he gat fperyng that a man 490
Off *Carrik*, that wes fley and wycht,
And a man als off mekill mycht,
As off the men off that countré
Was to the King ROBERT maift privé.
And he that wis his fib man ner, 495
And quhen he wald, forowtyn danger,
Mycht to the KINGS prefence ga.
Thar quheyr he, and hys fonnys twa,
War wonnand ftill in the cuntré,
For thai wald not perfawyit be, 500
That thai war fpeciall to the KING,
Thai maid hym mony tyme warnyng,

Quhen

Quhen that thai hys tynfaill mycht fe,
Forthy in thaim affyit he.
Hys name can I not tell perfay. 505
Bot Ik haiff herd fyndry men fay
That he wis the maift dowtit man
That in *Carrik* lewyt than.

And quhen Schyr INGRAME gat witting
Forfuth this wis na gabbing, 510
Eftyr hym in hy he fent;
And he come at hys cummandment.
Schyr INGRAME, that wis fley and wifs,
Tretyt with hym than on fic wyfs,
That he maid fekyr undirtaking 515
By trefoune for to flay the KING.
And he fuld haiff for hys feruice,
Giff he fullfillyt thair diuice,
Weill fourty pounds worth off land
Till hym, and till hys ayrs ay laftand. 520

The trefoune thus is undirtane;
And he hame till hys houfs is gane,
And wattyt opportunité
For to fullfill hys mawyté.

In gret perill than was the KING, 525
That off this trefoune wyft na thing.
For he, that he traifted maift of ane,
Hys dede falfly has undertane:

And

And nane may betreyſs tyttar than he
That man in trowis leawté.   530
The KING in hym traiſtyt: forthy
He had fullfillyt hys felouny,
Ne war the KING, throw Godds grace,
Gate hale witting off hys purchyace;
And how, and for how mekill land,   535
He tuk hys ſlauchtyr apon hand.

I wate not quha the warnyng maid;
Bot on all tyme ſic hap he had,
That quhen men ſchup thaim to be baiſs,
He gate witting tharoff alwayis.   540
And mony tyme, as I herd ſay,
Throw wemen, that he wyth wald play,
That wald tell all that thai mycht her.
And ſwa mycht happyn that it fell her.

Bot quhow that euir it fell, perdé,   545
I trow he ſall the warrer be.
Not forthy, the tratour ay
Had in hys thocht, bath night and day,
How he mycht beſt bring till ending
Hys treſounabill undertaking.   550

Ver. 542. Robert was, like Henry IV. of France, of an amorous compleƈtion, but even this his prudence turned to his intereſt, whereas Henry's would have ruined his affairs, if he had not been much indebted to fortune. Cæſar is alſo ſaid to have uſed Cupid's bow as a political machine.

Till he unbethinkand hym, at the laſt,
Intill hys hart gan undercaſt,
That the KING had in cuſtome ay
For to ryſs arly ilk day,
And paſs weill far from hys menye,   555
Quhen he wald paſs to the prewé,
And ſek a cowert hym allane;
Or at the maiſt with hym ane.
Thar thocht he, with hys ſonnys twa,
For to ſurpryſs the KING, and ſla.   560
And ſyne went to the wod thair way;
Bot yheit off purpoſs failit thai.
And not forthy thai come all thre
In a cowert, that wis priwé,
Quhar the KING oft wis wont to ga,   565
Hys priwé nedys for to ma.

    Thair hid thai thaim till hys cummyng.
And the KING, into the mornyng,
Raiſs quhen that hys liking wes,
And rycht towart that cowert gais,   570
Quhar liand war the tratours three,
For to do thar hys priueté.
To treſoun tuk he than na heid:
Bot he was wont, quhareuir he yeid,
Hys ſwerd about hys hals to ber;   575
And that awaillyt hym gretlé ther.

                                  For

Ver. 575. The long two-handed ſword was uſually hung round the neck, as its length forbad any other mode. In battle

For had not God all thing weldand
Sic help intill hys awyne hand,
He had bene dede, withowtyn dreid.
A chamber page thar with hym yeid.   580
And fwa, forowtyn falowis ma,
Towart the cowert gan he ga.

Now bot God help the nobill KING,
He is nerhand till hys ending.
For that cowert, that he yeid till,   585
Wes on the tothyr fid a hill,
That nane off hys men mycht it fe.
Thydderwart went hys page and he.
And he cummyn wes in the fchaw,
He faw the thre cum all on raw   590
Agaynis hym, full fturdely:
Than till hys boy he faid in hy,
" Yon men will flay us, and thai may.
" Quhat wapyn has yow?" ' Ha Schyr, perfay,
' I haiff bot a bow, and a wyr.'   595
" Giff me thaim fmertly bath." ' A! Schyr,
' How gate will you that I do?'
" Stand on fer and behald us to.
" Giff yow feis me abowyn be,
" Yow fall haiff wappynys gret plenté: 600
" And giff I dey withdraw yow fone."
With thir words, forowtyn hone,

battle the fhield was generally fufpended from the neck,
that both hands might be ufed in offence.
  Ver. 595. A *wyr* is an arrow.

He tite the bow owt off hys hand,
For the tratours wer ner cummand.
The fadyr had a fwerd bot mar; 605
The tothyr bath fwerd and hand ax bar;
The thred a fwerd had and a fper.
The King perfawyt, be thair affer,
That all wes as men had hym tauld.
" Traitour," he faid, " yow has me fauld. 610
" Cum na forthyr; bot hald thee thar.
" I will you cum na farthyr mar.'
' A! Schyr, unbethink yow,' faid he,
' How ner that I fuld to yow be.
' Quha fuld cum ner yow bot I?' 615
The KING faid, " I will fekerly
" That yow, at thys tyme, cum not ner;
" Yow may fay quhat yow will on fer."
Bot he, with fals words flechand,
Was with hys twa fonnys cummand. 620
Quhen the KING faw he wald not let,
Bot ay come on fenyeand falfet,
He taiffyt the wyir, and let it fley,
And hyt the fadyr in the ey,
Till it rycht in the harnys ran, 625
And he bakwart fell doun rycht than.
The brodyr, that the hand ax bar,
Swa faw hys fadyr liand thar,
A gyrd rycht to the King couth he maik,
And with the ax hym ourftraik. 630
Bot he, that had hys fwerd on hycht,
Roucht hym fic rout, in randoun rycht,

That

That he the hede till the harnyſs claiff,
And dede doun till the erd hym draiff.
The tothyr brodyr, that bar the ſper, 635
Saw hys brodyr fallin ther,
And with the ſper, as angry man,
With a raiſs till the KING he ran.
Bot the KING, that hym dred ſumthing,
Waytyt the ſper in the cummyng, 640
And with a wyſk the hed off ſtrak;
And or the tothyr had toyme to tak
Hys ſwerd, the King ſic ſwak him gaiff,
That he the hede till the harnys claiff.

He ruſchyt doun off blud all reid, 645
And quhen the KING ſaw thai war deid,
All thre lyand, he wepit his brand.
With that hys boy come faſt rynnand,
And ſaid, ' Our Lord mot lowyt be,
' That grauntyt yow mycht and powſté 650
' To fell the felny, and the prid,
' Off thir thre in ſwa litill tid.'
The KING ſaid, " Sa our Lord me ſe,
" Thai had bene worthy men all thre;
" Had thai not bene full off treſoun: 655
" Bot that maid thair confuſioun."

THE END OF BUKE V.

THE

THE
BRUCE.

BUKE VI.

ARGUMENT.

The KING *alane be nicht disconfits twa hundred Galwegians, and kills fourtein.—The poet feiling the miraculous hew of this tale, the onlie sik in his wark, gies a like ensampil fra Theban storie.— Prais of worship or curage.*—DUGLAS *kills* THIRLWALL.—*Schir* AYMER *de* VALLANGE, *and* JOHN *of* LORN, *advaunce again the King, quha retraits, but kills five of* LORN'S *men.*

THE
BRUCE.

BUKE VI.

THE KING is went till hys lodgyng.
And off this deid sone come tythyng
Till Schyr INGRAME the UMFRAWILL,
That thocht with sutelté, and with gyle,
Haid all failyeit in that place. 5
Tharfor anoyit swa he was,
That he agayne to *Lothyane*
Till Schyr AMER hys gate has tane.
And till hym tauld all hale the cass
That tharoff all for wondryt wass, 10
How ony man sa sodanly
Mycht do so gret chewalry,
As did the KING, that tyme allane
Wengeance off thre tratours has tane.
And said, " Certs I may weill se 15
" That it is all certanté
" That Hewyn helpys hardy men:
" As be this deid we may ken.
" War he not outrageouss hardy
" He had not unabasytly 20
" Sa

" Sa fmertly fene hys awantage.
" I drede that hys gret waffalage,
" And hys trawaill may bring till end
" That at men quhile full litill wend.

Sic fpeking maid he off the KING.   25
Quha ay, forowtyn fojournyng,
Trawaillyt in *Carrik*, her and thar,
His men fra hym fa fcalit war,
To purches thair neceffeté;
And als the countré for to fe;   30
That thai left not with hym fexty.
And quhen the *Gallowaifs* wyft futhli
That he wis with fa few mengye,
Thai maid a priwé affemblé
Off weill twa hundir men, and ma,   35
And flewth-hunds with thaim gan ta.
For thai thocht hym for to furprifs;
And giff he fled on ony wyfs,
To folow hym with the hunds fwa,
That he fuld not efchaip thaim fra.   40

Thai fchup thaim, in an ewynning,
To furpryfs fedanly the KING.
And till hym held thai ftraucht thair way.
Bot he, that had hys wachis ay
On ilk fid, off thair cummyng,   45
Lang or thai come, had wytting:
And how fele that thai mycht be.
Tharfor he thocht, with hys mengye,

To

To withdraw hym out off the place,
For the nycht weill fallyn was.   50
And for the nycht he thocht that thai
Suld not haiff ficht to hald the way,
That he war paffyt, with hys menye.
And as he thocht rycht fwa did he.
And went hym down till a morrafs,   55
Our a wattyr that rynnand was;
And in the bog he fand a place
Weill ftrait; that weill twa bow-drawcht was
Fra the wattyr, thai paffyt haid.
He faid, " Her may ye mak abaid,   60
" And reft yow all a quhill, and ly.
" I will ga wach all priuely,
" Giff Ik her oucht off thair cummyng;
" And giff I may her ony thing
" I fall ger warn you, fa that we   65
" Sall ay at our awantage be.

 The KING now takys hys gate to ga;
And with hym tuk he fergeands twa.
And Schyr GILBERT DE LE HAY left he
Thar, for to reft with hys menye.   70

 To the wattyr he come in hy,
And lyfnyt full ententily
Giff he herd oucht off thair cummyng:
Bot yheit mocht he her na thing.
Endlang the wattyr than yeid he   75
On aythyr fid gret quanteté,

         And

And faw the brayis hey ftandand,
The wattyr how throw flik rynnand:
And fand na furd that men mycht pafs,
Bot quhar hymfelwys paffit was.   80
And fwa ftrait wes the upcummyng,
That twa men mycht not famyn thring,
Na on na maner prefs thaim fwa,
That thai togyddir mycht lang to ga.

 And quhen he a langír quhill had bene thar, 85
He herknyt, and herd as it war
A hund's queftionyng on fer,
That ay come till hym ner and ner.
He ftude ftill, for till herkyn mar,
And ay the langer he wis thar,   90
He herd it ner and ner cummand;
Bot he thocht he thar ftill wald ftand,
Till that he herd mar takynnyng.
Than, for a hund's queftiounyng,
He wald not wakyn hys menye.   95
Tharfor he wald abid, and fe
Quhat folk thai war; and quhethir thai.
Held towart hym the rycht way;
Or paffyt ane othyr way fer by.
The moyne wis fchynand clerly;   100
Sa lang he ftude, that he mycht her
The noyis off thaim that cummand wer.

 Ver. 87. A hound's *quefting* is the eager yell he utters, when in *queft* of his prey.

         Then

Then hys twa men in hy send he
To warne, and wakyn hys menye.
And thai ar furth thair wayis gane; 105
And he left than all hym allane.
And swa stude he herknand,
Till that he saw cum at hys hand
The hale rout, intill full gret hy.
Than he unbethocht hym hastily 110
Giff he held towart hys menye,
That, or he mycht reparyt be,
Thai suld be passit the furd ilkane.
And than behuffyt he chofs ane
Off thir twa, othyr to fley or dey. 115
Bot hys hart, that wes stout and hey,
Consaillyt hym hym allane to bid,
And kep thaim at the furds sid;
And defend weill the upcummyng;
Sen he wes warnyst off armyng, 120
That he thair arowys hurt not dreid.
And giff he war off gret manheid,
He mycht stunay thaim euirlkane,
Sen thai ne mycht cum bot ane and ane.
And did rycht as hys hart hym bad. 125
Strang outrageoufs curage he had,
Quhen he sa stoutly, him allane,
For litill strenth off erd, has tane
To fecht with twa hunder and ma!
Tharwith he to the furd gan ga. 130

And thai, apon the tothyr party,
That faw hym ſtand thar anyrly,
Thrangand intill the wattyr rad,
For off hym littill dout thai had;
And raid till hym, in full gret hy.   135
He ſmate the fyrſt ſa wygoruſly
With hys ſper, that rycht ſcharp ſchar,
Till he doun till the erd hym bar.
The lave come then, intill a randoun,
Bot hys horſs, that wes born down,   140
Combryt thaim the upgang to ta.
And quhen the KING ſaw it wis ſwa,
He ſtekyt the horſs, and he gan flyng,
And ſyne fell at the upcummyng.

The laiff with that come with a ſchout;   145
And he, that ſtalwart wes and ſtout,
Met thaim rycht ſtoutly at the bra;
And ſa gud payment gan thaim ma,
That fyveſum in the furd he ſlew.
The lave then ſumdele thaim withdrew,   150
That dred hys ſtrakys wondre far,
For he in na thing thaim forbar.

Then ſaid ane, " Certs we ar to blame,
" Quhat ſall we ſay quhen we cum hame,
" Quhen a man fechts agayne us all?   155
" Quha wyſt euir men ſa foully fall
" As we, giff that we thus gat leve?"
With that all haile a ſchout thai geve;

And

And cryit, "On hym! he may not laſt!"
With that thai preſſyt hym ſa faſt,   160
That had he not the better bene,
He had bene dede withowtyn wen.
Bot he ſa gret defence gan mak,
That quhar he hyt ewyn a ſtrak,
Thar mycht na thing agayn ſtand.   165
In litill ſpace he left liand
Sa fele, that the upcummyn wes then
Dyttyt with ſlayn horſs and men.
Swa that hys fayis, for that ſtopping,
Mycht not cum to the upcummyng.   170

A! der God! quha had then bene by,
And ſene how he, ſa hardyly,
Addreſſyt hym againe thaim all,
I wate weill that thai ſuld hym call
The beſt that levyt in hys day.   175
And giff I the ſuth ſall ſay,
I herd neuir in na tyme gane
Ane ſtynt ſa mony hym allane.

Suth is quhen to ETHIOCLES
Fra hys brodyr POLNICES   180
                   Was

Ver. 179. The author, ſenſible that the ſtory he has juſt told has more the air of fable than any other incident of his work, attempts to vindicate it, by giving us a ſimilar exploit of Tydeus, from the Thebais of Statius, lib. ii. Statius was a favourite poet both with our author and with Chaucer, who, in his Houſe of Fame, puts Statius before Homer.

Was fend Thedeus in meſſage,
To aſk haly the heritage
Off *Thebes* till hald for a yer.
For thai twynis off a byrth wer,
Thai ſtrave, for ayther king wald be;   185
Bot the barnage off thair countré
Gert thaim aſſent on this maner,
That the tane ſuld be king a yer;
And then the toythir, and hys menye,
Suld not be fundyn in the toune,   190
Quhill the fyrſt brodyr regnand wer.
Syne ſuld the tothyr regne a yer;
And then the fyrſt leve the land,
Quhill the tothyr war regnand.
Thus ay a yer ſuld regne the tane;   195
The tothyr a yer fra that war gane.

To aſk halding off this aſſent
Wis Thedeus to *Thebes* ſent.
And ſwa ſpak for Polnices,
That off *Thebes* Ethiocles   200
Bad hys conſtabill with hym ta
Men armyt weill, and furth ga,

A better apology would have been that the panoply of a knight gave him vaſt advantage over a multitude ſlightly armed. When an army of French peaſants aroſe againſt the nobles, it is well known how few knights defeated them.

Ver. 190. This line rimes not, except by founding the firſt *e*. Editions read better:
   Suld not be found in that countrie.

To met Thedeus in the way,
And flay hym but langer delay.

The conftabill hys way is gane, 205
And nine and fourty with hym tane,
Swa that he with thaim maid fyfty.
Intill the ewennyng, priuely,
Thai fet enbufchement in the way,
Quhar Thedeus behowyt away 210
Betwix ane hey crag and the fe.
And he, that off thair mawyté
Wyft na thing, hys way has tane,
And towart gret bargane is gane.
And as he raid into the nycht, 215
Sa faw he, with the monys lycht,
Schynnyng off fcheldys gret plenté;
And had wondre quhat it mycht be.
With that all hale thai gaiff a cry,
And he, that hard fa fuddanly 220
Sic noyis, fum dele affrayit was.
Bot in fchort tyme he till hym taes
His fpyryts, full hardely;
For hys gentill hart, and worthy,
Affuryt hym into that nede. 225
Then with the fpurs he ftrak the fted,
And rufchyt in amang thaim all.
The fyrft he met he gert hym fall;
And fyne hys fwerd he fwappyt out,
And roucht about hym mony rout, 230

And flew fex-fum full fone, and ma;
Than under hym hys horfs thai flaw.
And he fell; but he fmertly raifs,
And ftrykand rowen about hym maifs;
And flew off thaim a quantité. 235
Bot wowndyt wondre far was he.

With that a litill rod he fand,
Up towart the crag ftrekand;
Thyddir went he, in full gret hy,
Defendand hym full douchtely, 240
Till in the crag he clam fumdell;
And fand a place enclofyt weill,
Quhar nane bot ane mycht hym affaill.
Thar ftud he, and gaiff thaim bataill;
And thai affaylyt euir ilkane; 245
And oft fell, quhen that he flew ane,
As he doun to the erd wald dryve,
He wald ber doun weill four or fyve.
Thar ftud he, and defendyt fwa,
Till he had flayne thaim half, and ma. 250
A gret ftane then by hym faw he,
That throw gret a mawyté,
Wes lowfyt redy for to fall.
And quhen he faw thaim cummand all,
He tumblyt doun on thaim the ftane; 255
And aucht men thar with it has flayne,
And fwa ftonayit the remanand,
That thai war weill ner retreand.

Then

Then wald he prifone hald na mar,
Bot on thaim ran with fuerd all bar.   260
And hewyt, and flew, with all hys mayn,
Till he has nine and fourty flayn.

The conftabill fyne gan he ta,
And gert hym fwer, that he fuld ga
Till King ETHEOCLES, and tell   265
The awentur that thaim befell.
THEDEUS bar hym douchtyly
That hym allane ourcome fyfty.

Ye, that this redys, cheyfs ye,
Quhethyr that mar fuld pryfit be   270
The KING, that, with awifement,
Undirtuk fic hardyment
As for to ftynt, hym ane, bot fer,
The folk that twa hunder wer;
Or THEDEUS that fuddanly,   275
For thai had raiffyt on hym the cry,
Throw hardyment that he had tane,
Wane fyfty men all hym allane.
Thai did thair deid baith on the nycht;
And faucht bath with the mone lycht.   280
Bot the KING difcomfyt ma;
And THEDEUS then ma gan fla.
Now demys quhethyr mar lowing
Suld THEDEUS haiff, or the KING.

In this manner, that Ik haiff tauld, 285
The KING, that ſtout wis and bauld,
Wis fechtand on the furd's ſyd,
Giffand and takand rowts reid.
Till he ſic martyrdom thar has maid,
That he the furd all ſtoppyt haid, 290
That nane off thaim mycht till hym rid;
Thaim thocht than foly for to byd;
And halely the flycht gan ta,
And went hamwarts quhar thai come fra.
For the KINGS men, with the cry, 295
Walknyt full affrayitly,
And come to ſek the lord thair KING.
The *Galloway-men* hard thair cummyng;
And fled, and durſt abid na mar.
The KINGS men, that dredand war 300
For thair lord, full ſpedyly
Come to the furd; and ſone in hy
Thai fand the KING ſyttand allane,
That off hys baſſynet has tane,
To awent hym, for he wis hate. 305
Then ſperyt thai at hym off his ſtate;
And he tauld thaim all haill the caſs,
Howgate that he aſſailyt was;
And how that God hym helpyt ſwa,
That he eſchapit hale thaim fra. 310

Then lukyt thai how fele war ded,
And thai fand lyand in that ſted
                    Fourtene,

Fourtene, that war flayne with hys hand.
Then louyt thai God faft, all weildand,
That thai thair lord fand hale and fer. 315
And faid thaim byrd on na maner
Dred thair fayis, fen thair chyftane
Wis off fic hart, and off fic mayne,
That he for thaim had undertane
With fwa fele for to fecht allane. 320

   Sic words fpak thai off the KING.
And for hys hey undertaking
Ferlyit, and yarnyt hym for to fe,
That with hym ay wes wont to be.

   A! quhat worfchip is perfyt thing! 325
For it mayfs men till haiff loving,
Giff it be folowit ythenly.
Bot pryce off worfchip not forthy
Is hard to wyn. For gret trewaill,
Oft to defend, and oft affaill, 330
And to be in thair deds wyfs,
Gers men off worfchip wyn the pryfs.
And may na man haiff worthyhed,
Bot he haiff wyt to fter hys deid;
And fe, quhat is to leve or ta. 335
Worfchip extremyteys has twa.
Fule-hardyment the formoft is,
And the tothyr is cowartyfs.
And thai ar bath for to forfak.
Fule-hardyment all will undertak, 340
Als

Als weill things to leve as ta.
And cowardyſs dois nathing ſwa;
Bot utterly forſakis all.
Bot that war wondir for to fall,
Na war faute off diſcretioun.   345
For this has worſchip ſic renoun,
That it is mene betwixt thais twa,
And takys that is till underta;
And levys that is to leve.   For it
Has ſa gret warniſhing off wyt,   350
That it all perills weile gan ſe,
And all awantage that may be.
I wald till hardyment hald haly,
With this away war foly;'
For hardyment with foly is wice.   355
Bot hardyment that mellyt is
With wyt, is worſchip; ay perdé,
For, bot wyt, worſchip may not be.

    This nobill KING, that we off red,
Mellyt all tyme with wyt manheid.   360
That may men by this mellé ſe;
Hys wyt ſchawyt hym the ſtrait entré
Off the furd, and the uſchyng alſua,
That, as hym thocht, wis hard to ta
Apon a man, that war worthy.   365
Tharfor hys hardyment haſtily
Thocht it mycht be weill undretane,
Sen at anys mycht aſſaill bot ane.

                             Thus

Thus hardyment gouernyt with wyt,
That he all tyme wald famyn knyt, 370
Gert hym off worfchip haiff the pryce;
And oft ourcum hys ennymyis.

The KING in *Carrik* duellyt ay ftill:
Hys men affemblyt faft hym till,
That in the land war trewailland, 375
Quhen thai off this deid herd tithand.
For thai thair ure wald with hym ta,
Gyff that he eft war affaylyt fwa.

Bot yeit the JAMES off DOWGLAS
In *Dowglafdaile* trawailland was, 380
Or ellys weill ner hand tharby,
In hyddillys fumdeill priuely.
For he wald fe hys gouerning,
That had the caftell in keping.
And gert mak mony juperty, 385
To fe quhethyr he wald ifche blythly.
And quhen he perfawyt that he
Wald blythly ifche with hys menye;
He maid a gadring priuely
Off thaim that war on hys party; 390
That war fa fele, that thai durft fycht
With THYRWALL, and all the mycht
Off thaim that in the caftell war.
He fchupe in the nycht to far.
To *Sandylands*: and ner tharby 395
He hym enbufchyt priuely,

And

And fend a few a trane to ma;
That fone in the mornyng gan ga,
And tuk catell, that wis the caftell by,
And fyne withdrew thaim haftily   400
Towart thaim that enbufchit war.
Than THYRWALL, forowtyn mar,
Gert arme hys men, forowtyn baid;
And ifchyt with all the men he haid:
And folowyt faft eftir the cry.   405
He wis armyt at poynt clenly,
Owtyn hys hede was bar:
Than, with the men that with hym war,
The catell folowit he gud fpeid,
Rycht as a man that had na dreid;   410
Till that he gat off thaim a fycht.
Than prekyt thai with all thair mycht,
Folowand thaim owt off aray;
And thai fped thaim fleand, quhill thai
Forby thair bufchement war paft: 415
And THYRWALL ay chaffyt faft,
And than thai that enbufchyt war
Ifchyt till hym, bath les and mar,
And rayffyt fudanly the cry.
And thai that faw fa fudandly   420
That folk come egyrly prikand
Rycht betwix thaim and thair warand,
Thai war into full gret effray.
And, for thai war owt off aray,
Sum off thaim fled, and fum abad.   425
And DOWGLAS, that thar with hym had

A gret

A gret menye, full egrely
Aſſaylyt, and ſcalyt thaim haſtily:
And in ſchort tyme ourraid thaim a,
That wiele nane eſchapyt thaim fra. 430

THYRWALL, that wis thair capitane,
Wis thar in the bargane ſlayne:
And off hys men the maiſt party.
The lave fled full effrayitly.

DOWGLAS hys menye faſt gan chaſs; 435
And the flears thair wayis tays
Till the caſtell, in full gret hy,
The formaſt entryt ſpedyly.
Bot the chaſſers ſped thaim ſa faſt,
That thai ourtuk ſum off the laſt, 440
And thaim forowtyn mercy gan ſla.
And quhen thai off the caſtell ſwa
Saw thaim ſla off thair men thaim by,
Thai ſparyt the yatts haſtily;
And in hy to the wallis rane. 445
JAMES off DOWGLAS' menye than
Seſyt weill haſtily in hand
That thai about the caſtell fand;
To thair reſett then went thair way.
Thus iſchyt THYRWALL that day. 450

Quhen THYRWALL on this maner
Had iſchit, as I tell yow her,

JAMES

JAMES off DOWGLAS, and hys men,
Buſkit thaim all ſamyn then,
And went thair way towart the KING   455
In gret hy; for thai herd tithing
That off WALENCE Schyr AMERY,
With a full gret chewalry,
Baith off *Scotts* and *Ingliſs men*,
With gret felny war redy then   460
Aſſemblyt for to ſek the KING,
That wis that tyme with hys gadring,
In *Cumnok*, quhar it ſtraitaſt was.
Thyddir then went JAMES off DOWGLAS;
And wis rycht welcum to the KING.   465
And quhen he had tauld that tithing,
How that Schyr AYMER wis cummand
For till hunt hym owt off the land
With hund and horne, rycht as he war
A woulff, a theyff, or theyffs fer.   470
Than ſaid the KING, " It may weill fall,
" Thoch he cum, and hys power all,
" We ſall abid in this cuntré;
" And giff he cummys we ſall hym ſe."

The KING ſpak apon this maner.   475
And off WALENCE Schyr AYMER
Aſſemblyt a gret cumpany
Off nobill men, and off worthy,

Ver. 463. Cumnock caſtle and village are in the moſt eaſtern part of Ayr-ſhire, near the head of the river Nith.
Ver. 476. About the month of April 1307.

Off

Off *Ingland*, and off *Lowthiane*.
And he has alsua with hym tane   480
IHONE off LORNE, and all hys mycht:
That had off worthy men, and wycht,
With hym aucht hundir men, and mae.
A slouth hund had he thar alsua,
Sa gud that change wald for nathing.   485
And sum men sayis yeit, that the KING
As a traytour hym noryst had,
And sa mekill off hym he maid,
That hys awyn hands wald hym feid.
He folowit hym quhareuir he yeid;   490
Sa that the hund hym folowit swa,
That he wald part na wyss hym fra.
Bot how that IHON off LORN hym had,
Ik herd never mentioun be mad.
Bot men sayis it wis certane thing   495
That he had hym in hys sesing;
And throw hym thocht the KING to ta;
For he wyst he hym luffyt swa,
That fra that he mycht anys fele
The KINGS sent, he wyst rycht weill   500
That he wald chaung it for na thing.
Thus IHON of LORNE hattyt the KING
For IHON CUMMYN hys emys sak.
Mycht he hym aythir sla, or tak,
He wald not pryss hys lyff a stra,   505
Sa that he wengeance off hym mycht ta.

The

The wardane then, Schyr AMERY,
With this IHONE in cumpany,
And othyrs of gud renoun alfua,
THOMAS RANDELL wis ane off tha, 510
Come intill *Cumnok* to fek the KING,
That wis weill war off thair cumming.
And wis up in the ftrenthys then,
And with hym weill four hundir men.
Hys brodyr that tyme with hym was, 515
And alfua JAMES off DOWGLAS.
Schyr AMERYS rowte he faw,
That held the plane ay, and the law;
And in hale bataill always raid.
The KING, that na fuppofyn had 520
That thai war ma than he faw thar,
To thaim, and nothyr ellys quhar,
Had ey; and wrocht unwittily.
For IHON of LORNE full futelly
Behind thocht to fuppryfs the KING. 525
Tharfor, with all hys gadring,
Aboute ane hill held the way,
And held hym into cowert ay;
Till he fa ner cum to the KING,
Or he perfawit hys cumming, 530
That he wis cummyn on hym weill ner.
The tothyr oft, and Schyr AYMER,

Ver. 510. Afterward the celebrated earl of Moray. He was the king's nephew; but in the Englifh intereft, and his bitter enemy for fome time after he was taken prifoner, fighting for his uncle's caufe, in the battle of Methven.

Preffyt

Preſſyt apon the tothyr party.
The KING was in gret japerty,
That wis on athyr ſid umbeſet 535
With fayis, that to ſla hym thret.
And the leyſt party off the twa
Was ſtarkar than he, and ma.

And quhen he ſaw thaim preſs hym to,
He thocht in hy quhat wis to do; 540
And ſaid, " Lords, we haiff na mycht,
" As at thys tyme to ſtand and fycht.
" Tharfor departs we in thre,
" All ſall not ſa aſſailyit be:
" And in thre parts hald our way." 545
Syne till hys priwé folk gan he ſay,
Betwix thaim into priueté,
In quhat ſted thair repayr ſuld be.

With that thair gate all ar thai gane,
And in thre parts thair way has tane. 550
IHONE off LORNE come to the place,
Fra quhar the KING departyt was.
And in hys trace the hund he ſet,
That then, forowtyn langer let,
Held ewyn the way eftir the KING, 555
Rycht as he had off hym knawing.
And left the tothyr partyſs twa,
As he na kep to thaim wald ta.
And quhen the KING ſaw hys cummyng,
Eftir his rowte intill a ling, 560

He thocht thai knew that it was he:
Tharfor he bad till hys menye
Yeit then in thre depertyt thaim fone;
And thai did fwa forowtyn hone;
And held thair way in thre partyfs. 565
The hund did thar fa gret maiftrys,
That held ay forowtyn changing,
Eftre the rowte quhar wes the KING.

And quhen the KING had fene thaim fwa
All in a rowte eftir hym ga, 570
The way, and folow nocht hys men,
He had a gret perfawyng then
That thai knew hym. For this in hy
He bad hys men rycht haftily
Scaile; and ilk ane hald hys way 575
All hymfelff; and fwa did thai.
Ilk man a fundry gate is gane.
And the KING with hym has tane
Hys foftyr brodyr, forowtyn ma,
And famyn held thar thai twa. 580

The hund folowyt alwayis the KING,
And changyt for na deperting;
Bot ay folowit the KINGS trace,
Bot waweryng, as he paffyt was.
And quhen that IHON off LORNE faw 585
The hund eftre hym draw,
And folow ftrak eftre thir twa,
He knew tha KING wis ane off tha.

        And

And bad fyve off hys cumpany,
That war rycht wycht men and hardy,   590
And als of fute spediast war,
Off all that in thair rowte war,
Ryn eftre hym, and hym ourta,
And lat hym nawyss pass thaim fra.

And fra thai had herd the bydding,   595
Thai held thair way eftre the KING.
And folowyt hym sa spedely,
That thai hym weill sone gan ourhy.
The KING, that saw thaim cummand ner,
Wis anoyit in gret maner,   600
For he thocht, giff thai war worthy,
Thai mycht hym trawaille and tarry,
And hald hym swa gate tariand,
Till the remanand com at hand.
Bot had he dred but anerly   605
Thaim fyve, I trow all sekyrly
He suld haiff had na mekill dred.
And till hys falow, as he yeid,
He said, " Thir fyve ar fast cummand:
" Thai ar weill ner now at owr hand.   610
" Sa is thar ony help at the?
" For we sall sone assaillyt be.'
' Ya Schyr,' he said, ' all that I may.'
" Yow sayis weill," said the KING, " persay.
" I se thaim cummand till us ner.   615
" I will na forthyr, bot rycht her

"I will

" I will byd, quhill it I am in aynd,
" And fe quhat force that thai can faynd."

 The K<small>ING</small> than ftud full fturdyly,
And the fyve-fum, in full gret hy   620
Come, with gret fchor and manaffing.
Then thre off thaim went to the K<small>ING</small>;
And till hys man the tothyr twa,
With fwerd in hand gan ftoutly ga.
The K<small>ING</small> met thaim that till hym focht; 625
And till the fyrft fic rowte he roucht,
That er and chek doune in the hals
He fchar, and off the fchuldrs als.
He rufhyt doun all difyly.
The twa that faw fa fudanly   630
Thair falow fall, effrayit war,
And ftert a litill owyr mar.
The K<small>ING</small> with that blenkit hym by,
And faw the twa-fome fturdily
Agane hys man gret mellé ma.   635
With that he left hys awyn twa,
And till thaim that faucht with hys man
A loup rycht lychtly maid he than;
And fmate the hed off the tane.
To mete hys awne fyne is he gane.   640
Thai cum on hym full fturdely:
He met the fyrft fa egrely,
That with the fwerd that fcharply fchar,
The arme fra the body he bar.

          Quhat

Quhat ſtrakys thai gaiff I cannot tell, 645
Bot to the KING ſa fayr befell,
That thoch he trewaill had and payne,
He off hys ſa men four has ſlayne.
Hys foſter brodyr thareſtir ſone
The fyrſt owt off dawys has done. 650

And when the KING ſaw that all fyve
War, in this wyſs, brocht owt of lyve,
Till hys falow than gan he ſay,
" Yow has helpyt weill, perſay."
' It likys yow to ſay ſwa,' ſaid he: 655
' Bot the gret pairt to yow tak ye,
' That ſlew four off the fyve, yow ane.'
The KING ſaid, " As the glew is gane,
" Better than yow I mycht it do,
" For Ik had mar layſer tharto. 660
" For the twa felowys, that delt with the,
" Quhen thai ſaw me aſſailyit with three,
" Off me rycht na kyn dout thai had;
" For thai wend I ſa ſtraytly war ſtad.
" And for this that thai dred me noucht, 665
" Noy thaim forout the mar I moucht."

With that the KING lukyt hym by,
And ſaw off LORNE the cumpany

Ver. 650. To *do owt of days* is to kill, as we ſay *to cut off his days*.

Weill ner, with the flouth hund cumand.
Than till a wod, that wis ner hand, 670
He went with his falow in hy.
God fayff thaim for hys gret mercy!

THE END OF BUKE VI.

THE
BRUCE.

BUKE VII.

ARGUMENT.

The KING *escapis to a wod. — Adventure of the thrie thieves.*—DOUGLAS *finds the* KING *in a hut. — With ane hundred and fiftie men thai disconfit part of Schir* AYMER's *host. — The* KING *kills thrie men—defeats Schir* AYMER *at Glentrule; after qubilk succefs attended him.*

THE BRUCE.

BUKE VII.

THE King towart the wod is gane,
Wery for fwayt, and will off wane.
Intill the wod fone entryt he;
And held doune towart a walé,
Quhar, throw the woid, a wattir ran;   5
Thydder in gret hy wend he than,
And begouth for to reft hym thar:
And faid he mycht ne forther mar.
His man faid, 'Schyr it may not be;
' Abyd ye her, ye fall fone fe   10
' Fyve hunder, yarnand yow to flaw;
' And thai ar fele aganys us twa.
' And, fen we may not dele with mycht,
' Help us all that we may with flycht.'
The King faid, " Sen that yow will fwa,   15
" Ga furth, and I fall with ye ga.
" Bot I haiff herd oftymys fay,
" That quha enlang a wattir ay,
" Wald waid a bow-draucht, he fuld ger
" Bathe the flouth hund, and hys leder,   20

" Tyne

" Tyne the flench men gret hym ta.
" Prowe we giff it will now do fa.
" For war yond diwilifs hund away,
" I roucht not off the lave perfay."

 As he dewifyt thai haiff doyn ;   25
And entryt in the wattir fone ;
And held down endlang thair way :
And fyne to the land yeid thai,
And held thair way, as thai did er.
And IHON of LORNE, with gret affer, 30
Come with hys route, rycht to the place,
Quhar that hys fyve men flayne was.
He menyt thaim quhen he thaim faw ;
And faid, eftre a litill thraw,
That he fuld wenge thair bloude.   35
Bot othyrwyfs the gamyn yowde.
Thar wald he mak na mar duelling ;
Bot furth in hy folowit the KING,
Rycht to the burn thai paffyt war.
Bot the flouth hund maid ftynting thar ; 40
And waweryt lang tyme, ta and fra,
That he na certane gate couth ga.
Till at the laft, that IHON of LORNE
Perfawit the hund the flouth had lorne :
And faid, " We haiff tynt this trawaill. 45
" To pafs forther may nocht awaill.
" For the woid is bath braid and wyd,
" And he is weill fer by this tyd.
          " Tharfor

" Tharfor is gud we turn agayne,
" And wayfte na mar trawaill in wayne."   50
With that relyt he hys mengé;
And hys way to the oft tuk he.

 Thus efchapyt the nobill KING.
Bot fum men fayis this efchaping
Apon an othyr maner fell,   55
Than throw the wading. For thai tell
That the KING a gud archer had;
And quhen hys Lord he faw fua ftad,
That he wis left fa anerly,
He ran on fyd allwayis hym by,   60
Till he into the woude wis gane.
Than faid he, till himfelff allane,
That he a reft rycht thar wald ma,
To luk giff he the hund mycht fla.
For giff the hund mycht left in lyve,   65
He wyft rycht weill that thai wald dryve
The KINGS trace, till thai hym ta.
Than wyft he weill tha wald hym fla.
And for he wald hys Lord fuccur,
He put hys lyff in awentur.   70
And ftud intill a bufk lurkand,
Till that the hund come to hys hand;
And with an arow fone hym flew;
And throw the woud fyne hym withdrew.
Bot quithyr this efchaping fell   75
As I tauld fyrft, or now I tell,

       I wate

I wate weill, without lefing,
That at the burn efchapit the KING.

The KING has furth hys wayis tane.
And IHON of LORNE agayne is gane   80
To Schir AYMER, that fra the chace
With hys men then repayryt was,
That fped litill thair chaffing;
Thocht that thai maid gret folowing,
Full egrely, thai wan bot fmall.   85
Thair fayis ner efchapyt all.
Men fayis Schyr THOMAS RANDELL than,
Chaffand, the KINGS baner wan.
Quharthrow in *Ingland* with the King
He had rycht gret price and lowing.   90

Quhen the chaffers relyit war,
And IHON of LORNE had met thaim thar,
He tauld Schyr AYMER all the cafe
How that the KING efchapyt wafe.
And how that he hys fyve men flew,   95
And fyne to the wode hym drew.
Quhen Schyr AMYR herd this, in hy
He fanyt hym, for the ferly:
And faid, " He is gretly to pryfs;
" For I knaw nane that lyffand is,   100
" That at myfcheyff gan help hym fwa:
" I trow he fuld be hard to fla,
" And he war bodyn ewenly."
On this wyfs fpak Schyr AMERY.

           And

And the gud KING held forth hys way, 105
Betwix hym and hys man, quhill thai
Paſſyt owt throw the foreſt war;
Syne in the more thai entryt thar.
It wis bathe hey, and lang, and braid;
And or thai halff it paſſyt had, 110
Thai ſaw on ſyd thre men cummand,
Lik to lycht men and wawerand.
Swerds thai had, and axys als;
And ane of thaim, apon hys hals,
A mekill boundyn wyddir bar. 115
Thai met the KING, and haliſt hym thar.
And the KING thaim thair halſying yauld;
And aſkyt quithyr thai wauld?
Thai ſaid, ROBERT the BRUYSS thai ſoucht;
For mete with hym giff that thai moucht, 120
Thair duelling with hym wald thai ma.
The KING ſaid, " Giff that ye will ſwa,
" Haldys furth your way with me,
" And I ſall ger yow ſone hym ſe."

Thai perſawit, be hys ſpeking, 125
That he wis the ſelwyn ROBERT King.
And changyt cuntenance, and late;
And held noucht in the fyrſt ſtate.

> Ver. 127. *Late* is geſture. *Lait, geſtus.* Iſl.
> And laſſes licht of *laittis.* Chriſt's Kirk.

For

For thai war fayis to the KING,
And thoucht to cum into fkulking; 130
And duell with hym, quhill that thai faw
Thair poynt, and bring hym tharoff daw.
Thai grantyt till hys fpek forthy.
Bot the KING, that wis witty,
Perfawit weill, be thair hawing, 135
That thai luffyt hym nathing.
And faid, " Falowis you mon, all three,
" Forthyr aqwent till that we be,
" All be your felwyn furth ga.
" And on the famyn wyfs we twa 140
" Sall folow behind, weill ner."
Quoth thai, ' Schyr it is na mifter
' To trow in us ony ill.'
" Nane do I," faid he; " bot I will,
" That yhe ga fourth thus, quhill we 145
" Better with othyr knawin be."
' We graunt,' thai faid, ' fen ye will fwa.'
And forth apon thair gate gan ga.

Thus yeid thai till the nycht wis ner.
And than the formaft cummand wer 150
Till a waift houfband houfs; and thar
Thai flew the weythir that thai bar.
And ftrak fyr for to roft thair mete;
And afkyt the KING giff he wald ete,
And reft hym till the mete war dycht. 155
The KING, that hungry was, Ik hycht,

Affentyt

Assentyt till thair spek in hy,
Bot he said he wald anerly
At a fyr; and thai all thre
On na wyss with thaim tillgyddre be.   160
In the end of the hous thai suld ma
Ane othyr fyr: and thai dyd swa.
Thai drew thaim in the hous end,
And halff the weythir till hym send.
And thai rostyt in hy thair mete;   165
And fell rycht freschly for till ete.
For the King weill lang fastyt had;
And had rycht mekill trawaill maid:
Tharfor he eyt full egrely.
And quhen he had etyn haftily,   170
He had to slep sa mekill will,
That he moucht set na let thartill.
For quhen the wanys fillyt ar,
Men worthys hewy euirmar;
And to slep drawys hewynes.   175
The KING, that all for trawaillit was,
Saw that hym worthyt slep nedways;
Till hys fostyr brodyr he sayis,
" May I traift in the, me to waik,
" Till Ik a litill sleping tak?"   180

 Ver. 158. Editions read,
    But he said he would alanerly
    Betwixt him and his fellow be
    At a fire; and they all three, &c.
The meaning is, that he and his man would have a fire
betwixt them, to themselves.

'Ya Schyr,' he said, ' till I may drey.'
The KING then wynkyt a litill wey;
And flepyt not full entrely;
Bot gliffnyt up oft fedanly.
For he had dreid off thaife thre men,   185
That at the tothyr fyr war then.
That thai hys fayis war he wyft;
Tharfor he flepyt, as foule on twyft.

The KING flepyt bot a litill than,
Quhen fic flep fell on his man,   190
That he mycht not hald up hys ey,
Bot fell in flep, and rowtyt hey.
Now is the KING in gret perille:
For flep he fwa a litill quhile,
He fall be ded, forowtyn dreid.   195
For the thre tratours tuk gud heid,
That he on flep wis, and hys man:
In full gret hy thai raifs up than,
And drew thair fuerds haftily;
And went towart the KING in hy,   200
Quhen that thai faw hym flepe fwa,
And flepand thocht thai wald hym fla.
The KING upblinkit haftily,
And faw hys man flepand hym by,
And faw cummand the tothyr thre.   205
Deliuerly on fute gat he;
And drew hys fwerd owt, and thaim mete.
And as he yeide hys fute he fet

       Apon

Apon hys man, weill hewily.
He waknyt, and raifs difsly: 210
For the flep maiftryt hym fwa,
That or he gat up ane off tha,
That come for to flaw the KING,
Gaiff hym a ftrak in hys ryfing,
Swa that he mycht help hym na mar. 215
The KING fa ftraitly ftad was thar,
That he wis neuir yheit fa ftad.
Ne war the armyng that he had,
He had bene dede, forowtyn wer.
Bot not forthy on fic maner 220
He helpyt hym, in that bargane,
That the thre tratours he has flane,
Throw Godds grace, and hys manheid.
Hys foftyr brodyr thar wis deid.
Then wis he wondre will off wayne, 225
Quhen he faw hym left allane.
Hys foftyr brodyr menyt he;
And waryit all the tothyr thre.
And fyne hys way tuk hym allane,
And rycht towart hys tryft is gane. 230

The KING went furth way, and angrely;
Menand hys man full tendrely.
And held hys way, all hym allane,
And rycht towart the houfs is gan,
Quhar he fet tryft to meit hys men; 235
It wis weill in with nycht be then.

VOL. I.　　　　O　　　　　　He

He come fone in the houfs, and fand
The houfswyff on the benk fittand,
That afkyt hym quhat he was,
And quhence he come, and quhar he gas. 240
" A trawailland man, dame," faid he,
" That trawaillys her throw the cuntré."
She faid, ' All that trewailland er,
' For ANE hys fak, ar welcum her.'
The KING faid, " Gud dame quhat is HE, 245
" That gers yow haiff fik fpecialté
" To men that trawaillis?" ' Schyr, perfay,'
Quoth the gud wyff, ' I fall yow fay;
' The KING, ROBERT the BRUYSS, is he,
' That is rycht lord off this cuntré. 250
' Hys fayis now hald hym in thrang;
' Bot I think to fe or echt lang,
' Hym lord and KING our all the land,
' That na fayis fall hym withftand.'
" Dame, luff yow hym fa weill?" faid he. 255
' Ya Schyr,' faid fche, ' fa God me fe!'
" Dame," faid he, " lo hym her yow by;
" For Ik am he, I fay the foithly."
' Ha!' faid the dame, ' and quhar ar gane
' Your men, quhen yow ar thus allane?' 260
" At this tyme, dame, Ik haiff na ma."
Sche faid, ' It may na wyfs be fwa.
' Ik haiff twa fonnys, wycht and hardy;
' Thai fall becum yowr men in hy.'

As

As sche deuisit thai haiff done. 265
Hys suorne men become thai sone.
The wyff syne gert hym syt, and ete.
Bot he has schort quhill at the mete
Syttyn, quhen he hard gret stamping
Abowt the houss. Then, but letting 270
Thai stert up, the houss for to defende.
Bot sone eftre the KING has kend
JAMES off DOWGLAS: then wis he blyth,
And baid oppyn the durs swyth:
And thai cum in, all that thar war. 275
Schyr EDUUARD the BRUCE wis thar;
And JAMES alsua off DOWGLAS,
That wis eschapyt fra the chace,
And with the KINGS brothyr met.
Syne to the traist that thaim was set 280
Thai sped thaim, with thair cumpany,
That war ANE HUNDIR and weill FYFTY.

And quhen that thai haiff sene the KING,
Thai war joyfull off thair meting.
And askyt how that he eschapyt was? 285
And he thaim tauld all hale the cass;
How the fyve men hym pressyt fast,
And how he throw the wattir past;
And how he met the thewis thre,
And how he slepand slane suld be, 290

Ver. 272. The narration is abrupt. Douglas surely spoke before the king knew him.

Quhen he waknyt, throw Godds grace;
And how hys foſtyr brodyr was
Slayne; he tauld thaim all haly.
Than lowyt thai God communly,
That thair lord wis eſchapyt ſwa. 295
Than ſpak thai words, ta and fra,
Till at the laſt the KING gan ſay,
" Fortoun us trawaillyt faſt to day,
" That ſcalyt us ſa ſedanly.
" Our fayis to nycht ſall ly traiſtly, 300
" Bot wachys, tak thair eſe and ly.
" Quharfor, quha knew thair herbery,
" And wald cum on thaim ſedanly,
" With ſew mengye, men mycht thaim ſcaith,
" And eſchaip forowtyn waith." 305
' Perfay,' quoth JAMES off DOWGLAS,
' As I come hyddyrwart, per caſs
' I come ſa ner thair herbery,
' That I can bring quhar thai ly.
' And wald yow ſpeid yow yheit or day 310
' It may ſwa happyn, that we may
' Do thaim a greter ſcaith weile ſone
' Than thai us all day has done.
' For thai ly ſcalyt, as thaim leſt.'
Than thoucht thaim all it wes the beſt 315
To ſpeid thaim to thaim haſtily.
And thai did ſwa in full gret hy,
And come on thaim, in the dawing,
Rycht as the day begouth to ſpring.

Sa fell it that a cumpany 320
Had in a toune tayn thair herbery,
Weile fra the oſt a myle, or mar.
Men ſaid that thai twa hundir war.
Thar aſſemblyt the nobill KING.
And ſone eftre thair aſſembling 325
Thai that ſlepand aſſayllyt war,
Rycht hidwyſly gan cry, and rar;
And other ſum, that herd the cry,
Raiſs ſa rycht effrayitly,
That ſum off thaim nakit war, 330
Fleand to warand, her and thar;
And ſum hys armys with hym drew.
And thai forowtyn mercy thaim ſlew.
And ſa crwyll wengeance gan ta,
That the twa parts of thaim, and ma, 335
War ſlayne, rycht in that ilk ſted.
Till thair oſt the remanand fled.

The oiſt that hard the noyis and cry,
And ſaw thair men ſa wrechytly,
Sum nakit, fleand her and thar, 340
Sum all hale, ſum wawndyt ſar;
Into full gret effray thai raiſs,
And ilk man till hys baner gayis.
Swa that the oyſt wes all on ſter.
The KING, and thai that with hym wer, 345
Quhen on ſter the oyſt ſaw ſwa,
Towart thair warand gan thai ga.

And thar in faweté come thai.
And quhen Schyr AYMER herd fay
How that the KING thair men had flayne; 350
And how thai turnyt war agayne;
He faid, 'Now may we clerly fe
' That nobill hart, quhar euir it be,
' It is hard till ourcum with mayftry.
' For quhar an hart is rycht worthy 355
' Agayne ftoutnes it is ay ftout.
' Na, as I trow, thar may na dowte
' Ger it all owt difcomfyt be,
' Quhill body lewand is and fre.
' As be this mellé may be fene. 360
' We wend ROBERT the BRUCE had bene
' Swa difcumfyt, that be gud fkill
' He fuld neuir haiff haid hart, ne will,
' Swilk juparty to underta.
' For he put was at undre fwa 365
' That he was left all hym allane,
' And all hys folk war fra hym gayn.
' And he fa gat for trawaillyt,
' To put thaim off that hym affailyt,
' That he fuld haiff yarnyt refting 370
' This nycht, atour all othyr thing.
' Bot hys hart fillyt is off bounté,
' Swa that it wencufyt may not be.'

On this wyfs fpak Schyr AMERY.
And quhen thai off hys cumpany 375
Saw

Saw how thai trawaillyt had in wayn,
And how the KING thair men had flayn,
And that hys men wes gane all fre;
Thaim thocht it was a niceté,
For to mak thar longer duelling,   380
Sen thai mycht not anoy the KING.
And said fua to Schyr AMERY;
That unbethocht hym haftely
That he to *Carlele* wald ga,
A quhill tharin fojourn ma,   385
And haiff hys fpyis on the KING,
To knaw alwayis hys cuntenyng.
And quhen that hys poynt mycht fe,
He thocht that, with a gret menȝe,
He fuld fchute apon hym fedanly.   390
Tharfor, with all hys cumpany,
Till *Ingland* he the way has tane,
And ilk man till hys houfs is gane.

In hy till *Carlele* went is he.
And tharin thinkis for till be,   395
Till he hys poynt faw off the KING;
Quha then with all hys gadring
Wis in *Carryk*, quhar he was wont,
He wald went with hys men till hunt.

Sa happynyt that, on a day,   400
He went till hunt, for till affay

Ver. 379. *Niceté* is folly, perhaps from the French *niais*.
    The meffage was not *nice*.   Shak. Rom. and Jul.

Quhat gamyn wis in that cuntré.
And swa hapnyt that day that he
By a woud-syd to hunt is gane,
With hys twa hundys hym allane.   405
Bot he hys suerd ay with hym bar.
He had but schort quhill sittyn thar,
Quhen he saw fra the woud cumand
Thre men, with bowys in thair hand,
That towart hym come spedely.   410
And he that persawyt that in hy,
Be thair affer and thair hawing,
That thai luffyt hym na kyn thing;
He raiss, and hys leysche till hym drew he,
And leyte hys hunds gan all fre.   415

God help the KING now, for hys mycht!
For bot he now be wyss and wycht,
He sall be set in mekill press.
For thir thre men, forowtyn less,
War hys fayis all uterly.   420
And wachyt hym sa besyly,
To se quhen thai wengeance mycht tak
Off the KING, for IHON CUMYN his sak.

And thai thocht than thai leysur had;
And, sen he hym allane wes stad,   425
In hy thai thocht thai suld hym sla.
And giff that thai mycht chewyss sa,
Fra that thai the KING had slayne,
That thai mycht wyn the woud agayn,

Hys

Hys men thaim thocht thai fuld not dreid. 430
In hy towart the KING thai yeid,
And bent thair bowys, quhen thai war ner;
And he, that dred on gret maner
Thair arowys, for he nakyt was,
In hy a fpekyng to thaim maes. 435
And faid, " Yow oucht to fchame, pardé,
" Sen Ik am ane, and yow ar thre,
" For to fchute at me apon fer.
" Bot had ye hardyment to cum ner,
" And with your fuerds till affay, 440
" Wyn me apon fik wyfs giff ye may,
" Ye fall weill owte mar prefyt be."
' Perfay,' quoth ane then off the thre,
' Sall na man fay we dreid ye fwa,
' That we with arowys fall ye fla.' 445

With that thair bowys away thai keft,
And come on faft, but langer freft.
The KING thaim mete full hardyly,
And fmate the fyrft fa wigoruſly,
That he fell dede doun on the gren. 450
And quhen the KINGS hund has fene
Thaife men affaillie hys maifter fwa;
He lap till ane, and gan hym ta
Rycht be the nek, full fturdely,
Till top our tale he gert hym ly. 455
And the KING, that hys fuerd oute had,
Saw he fa fayr fuccur hym maid,

Or

Or he that fallyn wis mycht ryſs,
He hym aſſaillyt on ſik wyſs,
That he the bak ſtrak ewyn in twa.   460
The thryd, that ſaw hys falowis ſwa,
Forowtyn recowering, be ſlayne,
Tuk to the wode hys way agayne.
Bot the KING folowit ſpedyly;
And als the hund, that wes hym by,   465
Quhen he the man ſaw fle hym fra,
Schot till hym ſone, and gan hym ta
Rycht be the nek, and till hym dreuch.
And the KING, that wis ner eneuch,
In hys ryſſing ſik rowt hym gaff,   470
That ſtane dede to the erd he draff.

The KINGS men war than ner,
Quhen that thai ſaw, on ſik maner,
The KING aſſailyt ſa ſedanly,
Thai ſped thaim towart hym in hy.   475
And aſkyt how that caſs befell?
And he all haly gan thaim tell,
How thai aſſailyt hym all thre.
'Perfay,' quoth thai, ' we may weill ſe
' That it is hard till undertak   480
' Sic melling with yow to mak,
' That ſa ſmertly has ſlayn thir thre,
' Forowtyn hurt.' " Perfay," ſaid he,
" God, and my hund, has ſlayn the twa,
" The thryd eſchapyt nocht alſua;   485
                                    " Thair

" Thair tresoun cumbryt thaim persay,
" For rycht wycht men all thre war thai."

 Quhen that the KING, throw Godds grace,
On this maner eschapyt was,
He blew hys horne, and then in hy   490
Hys gud men till hym gan rely.
Than hamwarts buskyt he to far,
For that day wald he hunt ne mar.

 In *Glentruell* a quhill he lay;
And went weill oft to hunt and play,   495
For to purches thaim venesoun,
For than der war in sesoun.

 In all that tyme Schyr AMERY,
With nobill men in cumpany,
Lay in *Carlele*, hys poynt to se.   500
And quhen he hard the certanté,
That in *Glentruell* wis the KING,
And went till hunt, and till playing,
He thoucht, with hys chewalry,
To cum apon hym sedanly.   505

Ver. 502. The wood of Glentrule is in the eastern part of Ayrshire.

Sir Aymer de Vallange, earl of Pembroke, advanced to encounter Bruce in June 1307, as would seem. The death of Edward, 7 July, appears to have been one cause that his measures became embarrassed, and unsuccessful.

             And

And fra *Carlele* on nychts ryd;
And in cowert on dayis byd.
And fwa gate, with fyk tranenting,
He thoucht he fuld furpryfs the KING.
He affemblyt a gret mengye   510
Off folk off full gret renouné,
Bath off *Scotts* and *Inglis men*.
Thair way all famyn held thai then,
And raid on nycht fwa priuely,
Till thai come in a wod, ner by   515
Glentruele, quhar logyt wis the KING,
That wyft rycht nocht off thair cumming.

  Into gret perille now is he,
For bot God, throw hys gret powfté,
Save hym, he fall be flayne or tane, 520
For thai war fex quhar he wis ane.

  Quhen Schyr AMERY, as Ik haiff tauld,
With hys men, that war ftout and bauld,
War cummyn fwa ner the KING, that thai
War bot a myle fra hym away;   525
He tuk awifement with hys men,
On quhat maner thai fuld do then.
For he faid thaim that the KING was
Logyt into fa ftrayt a place,
That horfs-men mycht not hym affaile. 530
And giff fute-men gaiff hym bataille,
He fuld be hard to wyn, giff he
Off thair cummyn may wittyt be.
                                     'Tharfor

'Tharfor I rede all priuely
'We fend a woman, hym to fpey,   535
'That powerly arrayit be.
'Sche may afk mete per cheryté;
'And fe thair cowyn halily,
'And apon quhat maner thai ly.
'The quhill we, and owr menye,   540
'Cummand owt throw the wod may be
'On fute, all armyt as we ar.
'May we do fwa, that we cum thar
'On thaim, or thai wyt our cummyng,
'We fall find in thaim na fturting.'   545

This cunfaill thocht thaim wis to beft.
Then fend thai furth, bot langer freft,
The woman, that fuld be thair fpy.
And fche her way gan hald in hy
Rycht to the loge quhar the KING,   550
That had na dred off furpryffing,
Yeid unarmyt, mery and blyth.
The woman has he fene alfwyth.
He faw hyr uncouth; and forthy
He beheld her mar entrely.   555
And be hyr cuntenance hym thocht'
That for gud cummyn was fche nocht.

Then gert he men in hy hyr ta.
And fche, that dred men fuld hyr fla,
Tauld how that Schyr AMERY,   560
With the CLYFFURD in cumpany,

With

With the flour off *Northummyrland*,
War cummand on thaim at thair hand.

 Quhen that the KING herd that tithing,
He armyt hym, bot mar duelling.   565
Sa did thai all that euir was thar;
Syne in a sop assemblyt ar.
I trow thai war THRE HUNDER ner.
And quhen thai all assemblyt wer,
The KING hys baner gert display,   570
And set hys men in gud aray:
Bot thai had standyn bot a thraw
Rycht at thair hand quhen that thai saw
Thair fayis, throw the wod cummand,
Armyt on fute, with sper in hand;   575
That sped thaim full enforcely.
The noyis begouth sone, and the cry.
For the gud KING, that formast was,
Suttely towart hys fayis gayss,
And hynt owt off a manys hand,   580
That ner besid hym was gangand,
A bow, and ane arow braid als;
And hyt the formast in the hals,
Till thropill and wesand yeid in twa,
And he doun till the erd gan ga.   585

 The laiff with that maid a stopping.
Than, bot mar bad, the nobill KING
Hynt fra hys baneour hys baner;
And said, " Apon thaim! for thai ar
          " Discomfyt

" Discomfyt all!" With that word 590
He swappyt swyftly owt hys swerd,
And on thaim ran sa hardely,
That all thai off hys cumpany
Tuk hardyment off hys gud deid.
For sum, that fryst thair wayis yeid, 595
Agayne come to the fycht in hy,
And mete thair fayis wigorusly;
That all the formast ruschyt war.
And thai that war hendermar
Saw that the formast left the sted, 600
Thai turnyt sone thair bak, and fled.
And owt off the wod thaim withdrew.
The KING a few men off thaim slew,
For thai rycht sone thair gate gan ga.
It discomfortyt thaim al sua 605
That the KING, with hys mengye, was
All armyt to defend that place,
That thai wend, throw thair trawenting,
Till haiff wonyn, forowtyn fychting.
That thai effrayit war sedanly; 610
And he thaim foucht sa angrely,
That thai in full gret hy agayne
Owt off the wod, rane to the playne:
For thaim faillyt off thair entent.
Thai war that tyme sa foully schent, 615
That fyften hunder men, and ma,
With a few mengye war rebotyt swa,
That thai withdrew thaim schamfully.
Tharfor amang thaim sedanly

Thar

Thar raifs debate, and gret diftance, 620
Ilk ane wyte othyr off thair myfchance.
Clyffurd and Wauss maid a mellé,
Quhar Clyffurd roucht hym routs thré.
And aythir fyne drew till partyfs.
Bot Schyr Amer, that wis wyfs, 625
Departyt thaim with mekill payn.
And went till *Ingland* hame agayn.
He wyft, fra ftryff rafs thaim amang,
He fuld thaim not held famyn lang,
Forowtyn debate or mellé; 630
Tharfor till *Ingland* turnyt he.
With mar fchame than he went off town;
Quhen fa mony, off fic renoun,
Saw fa few men bid thaim bataill,
Quhar thai ne war hardy till affaill. 635

Ver. 632. The expreffion bears a proverbial appearance; the *town* may be Carlile.

END OF THE FIRST VOLUME.

www.ingramcontent.com/pod-product-compliance
Lightning Source LLC
Chambersburg PA
CBHW021826230426
43669CB00008B/874